THERE IS
SUNSHINE
AFTER THE RAIN

Making It Through Life's Struggles

PATRICIA A. SAUNDERS

ISBN: 978-1-54391-866-3 (print)
ISBN: 978-1-54391-867-0 (ebook)

DEDICATION

This book is dedicated to my parents, Rev. Betty L. Saunders and Oscar A. Saunders, Sr., for loving me, teaching me about faith, and showing me that it's okay to forgive in order to receive my blessings.

To my siblings: who each helped me pick up the pieces when I fell apart. They stepped in to fill the spaces where there was a hole. The daily calls, prayers, and encouragement to continue on when I wanted to quit.

To my nieces and nephews: when I needed to dance, turned up the music. When I felt down and needed a hug, opened their arms. When I traveled bicoastal to stay connected to my roots, shared memories, laughs, and gave me the kiss around my neck.

To my favorite cousin, Shirley McKinnon, who stepped in as my second mother after the passing of my mother. When I needed to vent, she answered the phone and listened. She also sent me pictures from my childhood to remind me that I was always loved, no matter what.

To my teams that keep me motivated and focused. I would be lost without you. Marketing: Ella D. Curry, for hosting my books on tour, posting on social media, and keeping them in front of the readers. Promotional team: LaShaunda Hoffman and Amber Childress, for keeping me up to date with social media and making my job easier. Proofreader: Paulette Nunlee. Web Master: Kenneth Ngai, who rolled up his sleeves and developed my website, made numerous changes until it was perfect, and worked tirelessly before his honeymoon to make sure it was live. Photographer: Eric Gerald Marshall. To my volunteers who assist me at all my book signings, thank you.

Lastly, to my readers: I appreciate your loyal support and I thank you from the bottom of my heart.

INTRODUCTION

"And he shall be as the light of the morning, when the sun riseth, even a morning without clouds; as the tender grass springing out of the earth by clear shining after rain".

The funeral service is over, everyone has gone back to their places, and you're left alone. You were the caregiver, you memorized the medical records, and now you are disorganized. The world has swallowed you up and spit you out.

Sitting there with the pieces of your life around you, there seemed to be a pattern. There was faith, love, deceit, lust, and loss—in that order. You didn't think you were deserving of love. That is why everything was being taken from you, and you were ready to give up on life.

Through your poetry, faith, and learning from your past, you can rewrite the story. It was after coming through all the experiences and being stronger, you realized there is always a new chapter.

The book will take you on the journey of a young girl growing up in Connecticut, who had to take some stumbles along the way to come into her own and realize instead of tearing herself down for the decisions she made, there is a lesson. Love is greater than anyone can imagine and can warm you like the sunshine after the rain.

You went from the beginning, the journey, the test, and the testimony to say, "There Is Sunshine after the Rain."

CONTENTS

DEDICATION..v

INTRODUCTION vi

In The Beginning...1

Grieving You..2

He Leadeth Me Beside Still Waters...4

Ain't No Mountain High Enough 5

I Am Not The Woman I Used To Be..6

Too Old For Games 7

Looking For A Mr. Do Right 8

I'm Staying 9

Why Jump In The Puddle?...10

Mister..11

Penny For Your Thoughts 12

Blue Cadillac 13

Eight Years 15

I Cried For You..17

Promises Are Meant To Be Broken..19

I Want To Hurt You 20

Forgiveness...21

Roots...23

Advice To My Daughters 24

The Womb...26

If I Had Wings I Could Fly 28

Another One Bites The Dust 29

The Stage Is Set 30

Momma Used To Say..31

Hold On..32

Move 33

INTERLUDE 34

The Beginning 35

PART 2..37

Daddy's Girl 37

Bus Stop...39

Not A Day Goes By 40

A Mother's Love 42

Gone 43

The Answer 44

LET GO 45

It's Hard Being A Girl 46

Romeo and Juliet 47

Turn Back The Hands of Time 48

Up North 49

Dreams Do Come True 50

There Something About You 51

Like an Onion 52

Learning to Love Again 53

The First Meeting 54

24 Hours 55

How Deep Is Your Love? 56

My Gift To You 57

With This Ring 58

INTERLUDE 59

The Journey 60

PART 3 67

Take The Hint 67

I Would Have Freed More If They Only Knew 68

You Can't Control A Free Spirit 69

You Can Wake Me 70

Where Would I Be? 71

Time 72

Glory 73

Be Somebody 74

Do You Know What You Want? 75

Goodbye To The Past 76

A Shot Rings Out 77

Momma's Nightgown 78

Close Your Eyes 79

My Letter To Theo 80

Don't Forget 83

Exclamation Point 84

Appreciate My Thickness 85

He Will Restore 86

Weak In The Knees 87

BABY MOMMA 88

Feed Me 90

Strawberries And Cream 91

Please Me 92

INTERLUDE 93

The Test 94

PART 4 101

Touch Me 101

It Was Worth The Wait 103

Sing Me A Lullaby 104

Spending Time With You 105

He Speaks To Me 106

Knight In Shining Armor 107

The Will 108

74 Columbia Boulevard 109

Yesterday 111

Guardian Angel 113

It's Raining... 114

With My Hands Up.. 116

My Body Is Calling 118

I Smell Her 119

P.I.M.P. 120

Dear God.. 121

Acceptance 123

It's 2 A.M. 124

Curious... 125

Give Me Strength 127

A Brighter Day 128

It's Back.. 129

He Won't Answer 130

INTERLUDE 131

The Testimony 132

PART 5... 143

You Will One Day Understand 143

One Wish 144

I Rise Up 145

The Message 146

The Wedding 147

Love Over Everything 149

I Made A Mistake 150

Something for Boom Boom Room 151

Keep Living 154

Put Respect on My Name 155

Sometimes It Hurts 156

Being Alone 157

It's Here 158

Saving The Cookies 159

Cabo 160

Ten Years 161

Scab 163

Plus 1 165

Happy Anniversary 166

It's Almost a Year 167

Another Angel Got Their Wings 168

Let Me Drink Your Bath Water 169

Knocking At The Door 170

Stop Waiting 171

Bargaining 172

They Don't Know 173

Redbone 175

Loving Me 176

Prisoner in My Mind 177

Texting 178

Dress Rehearsal 179

There Is Sunshine After The Rain 180

CONCLUSION 182

RESOURCES 184

Signs Of Dementia 185

Steps Of Grieving 186

Signs that you are dating a married man 187

Surviving Working In A Hostile Work Environment 188

Bibliography 189

About the Author 190

In The Beginning

Where to begin?
I can remember as a child, laughter
Playing in the backyard
The neighborhood kids would come
We would play tag
Running with not a care in the world
Running to the corner store
Buying penny candy
On hot summer days there was the little plastic pool
Putting on bathing suits and splashing around
I could hear my mother in the house
Pots clanging
Seeing my father on the front porch reading the paper and watching cars going by
Those were the good days
You had to be in the house before dark
Anxious to wash my hands and prepare for dinner
Sitting around the table
Listening to adult conversations
Speaking when spoken to
Watching the *Lawrence Welch Show* together
We were a family
We were happy

Grieving You

It's been thirteen years
Secrets
Lovemaking
You're my best friend
My friends think you're imaginary
Yet you're real
You came to my home every week
We talked every day. You're the first voice I heard and the last one at night.
We made love
We talked about the future
You shared your dreams with me
I told you my thoughts that I couldn't share with others
I knew what you wanted me to know
This goes on for years
No commitment
I was my married friends' envy because it's everything a girl wants
My single friends ask me questions
They want to know what the arrangements are:
Is it fair to not be in a relationship?
How do you know he's not married?
Have I checked public records?
Is it fair to you?
I say I am fine with it
I lied
No holidays, no weekends, no nights?
Well there were some
It wasn't until the questions were asked
What about the kids you could have had?
What about the events you could have gone to as a couple?
What about what you want?

I stood there
Lump in my throat and I had to admit
I was settling
So I prayed if it is meant to be…

The phone calls stopped
The visits stopped
I was puzzled and thought if he loved me
Why is he not calling?
Why is he not coming over?
I grieved you
I missed your touch
I missed the love that I thought we shared
I whispered goodbye to the wind, hoping that you would hear
Today I admitted that I grieved you

He Leadeth Me Beside Still Waters

With life being so hectic
I was drawn to the water
I sat there and wept
Not sad tears, but tears of joy
I am blessed to be alive
I had to look at all he has brought me through
I looked at my surroundings
The butterfly touching the flowers
The gecko running in the sand to get to the right hot spot to sun
A light breeze against my skin
God, you brought me here to paradise to hear you talk to me

As your child, I am listening
Always running to catch something
Deadlines to meet
Reservations to respond to…
I had to stop!
I am taking care of myself
I am letting go of the negative
I only have one life to live
I want to smell my flowers
I want to see my sunsets
I want to feel the grass between my toes

Ain't No Mountain High Enough

Life has created stumbling blocks
They pile up as high as a mountain
On my own I keep trying to climb over each mountain:

- Work
- Relationships
- Family
- Friends

As I get to another level of this journey, life piles on another block
I give up
I surrender
At that moment, I feel like I am losing it
Everything that I care about is being taken away
It takes time to heal
I realize that not everything I was holding onto was meant for me
I am free from everything
Everything is clearer
I make a point of wanting to share with my legacy that we come from strong
women
Women who put their faith first to make it through everything from segregation,
inequality, and colorism.
They believed that a better day was coming and that the struggle would not last.
I can hear them whisper "Baby, ain't no mountain high enough that you can't
climb."
You can do it!

I Am Not The Woman I Used To Be

I am half a century years old

I keep encountering souls who are stuck in the 80s

I have gone through many storms

Not all written, but the scars are still there

I have had people joke about my past

I have had people who I love take out their insecurities on me

I have had people distance themselves because

I am not the woman I used to be

The life of the party doesn't mean to belittle me

The life of the party means a good life, but not at my expense

When you throw up things from my past and I stare blankly at you

I don't recognize who you are

I am here in the moment, and you're still in the past

I have had people ask, "why are you still single"?

Like it's a sentence in jail.

I am looking at some who are cheating, complaining about their spouses, or worse

I have had some say, "I would never live here"

Fast forward years later you're living exactly where I lived, how I lived, and I moved on

I might not say anything, I just distance myself like you do, and I shake my head because

I am not the woman that I used to be

Too Old For Games

I experimented and tried something new
Online Dating is the new fad
You post a picture
People make up stuff they feel you want to hear
You get likes and flirts
So, I said let me try this
My friends encouraged me to open my heart
Being single for a long period of time, you're set in your ways
So the person and I exchange emails
We then decide to chat
Seems like it might be a match
There is something that is nagging me
Pushed it back and said to myself I was just being too cautious

We talked some more and I am listening
It's like my ears are on fire because I hear everything
There it is… a slip
My tone in my voice changed
He caught it afterwards
We end the conversation politely
Later I get the Dear Johnette text
I respond back and I state
I am too old for games

Looking For A Mr. Do Right

Talking to others about what they are looking for in a mate
I get the list
Tall, Dark and Handsome
Suggestion is to dig deeper
If this is going to be a relationship that lasts, don't you want something more?
They break out in a laugh
Honey, I want a Mr. Do Right
Puzzled I must look
Mr. Do Right will be home at a reasonable time
He will open doors
He won't worry about who is paying the tab when you go out
He's a gentleman
Mr. Do Right will have no problem expressing his affection towards you
He won't have a wandering eye for your friends or the neighbor next door
I started smiling
They were in unison, clapping like they know he's coming
They said if Mr. Do Right walks in the door right now, it's something that lets you
know it's him
You don't have to question it.
He respects you
The only person he puts before you is God
I pulled up a chair and started clapping, too
I want a Mr. Do Right!

I'm Staying

As the sun sets high in the sky

There is always going to be breakfast on the table

Coffee brewing

Hot water running in the shower

And my sugar!

See he makes me feel indispensable

He awakes me with a low song of good morning in my ear

His touch to my skin makes me smile

Yeah, he's my sugar!

We shower together

Why waste the water

He dries me off first

I return the favor

As the steam evaporates from the mirror you see love looking back

He's my sugar!

Now the road hasn't always been easy

There were times when we wanted to let go

We remembered that it's until death do us part

We got to work at it like we were getting paid

Like our lives depended on it

Am I leaving?

No! I'm staying

Why Jump In The Puddle?

It's raining hard outside
It subsides, and we run to put on our coats and boots
First one out the door is giggling
Mommy screams from the front porch, "Don't jump in"
Too late!
We are jumping, singing, and feeling the sprinkle of rain on our faces
We are not having a care in the world
No one is thinking about rent, car notes, and bills.
We're kids
The innocence of being adventurous
The desire to get wet, dirty, and have fun
When did it change?
As we became teenagers and became more concerned about our appearance
Don't step on my Air Force 1's
Go back to that child who didn't care
Go back to that feeling
Jumping, stomping, and feeling that water splash all over us
We came back in happy
Soaked and having to undress quickly before we caught a cold
It was something about seeing the puddle of water
That drew us in and made us jump!

Mister

He was very sweet

Everyone loved him

I thought of him as a friend and would hug him whenever I saw him

Circumstances changed beyond my control, and he became my master.

His game plan was to break me

You were loyal to your other owner

He examines me, and explained that I cost too much

Was I worth what he had paid?

My eyes welled up

Sir, I will do whatever you want

Humiliation in front of others is what I had to endure

If they did something wrong, I took the beating

I wanted to run away, but fear of where would I go

I tried to see if others would have me

Mister called in backup, and his boss looked at me with disgust

You're going to stay here

Daily I would come to the plantation as I called it

I would do what was expected, and it was never good enough

He had the other servants reporting on my actions

Mister said it's nothing personal, it's business!

I had no one to protect me. I had no rights! Until the skies opened up

I ran as far as I could and I was free!

Penny For Your Thoughts

I have a penny
A shiny penny
I am wondering what your thoughts are
Well my thoughts are about the world
Why are we killing each other?
Why is there always on the news that someone is taking another person's life?
I have questions about global warming
Are we living in our last days?
If so, why are we not all enjoying each moment?
Why are we always complaining?
We complain about bills
The weather isn't right
The stock market isn't returning on investments for us
We complain about our looks
Life is too short!
Did our forefathers sacrifice for nothing?
Did we have people unknown to us make a protest so that we can be free?
So it's going to take more than a penny
I want to know why when I look into someone's eyes that I see hate
Don't we all pray?
Don't we know that we should treat those as we want to be treated?
But why?

Blue Cadillac

This was my introduction to the big ride
She came home excited
We all ran outside to look at her new ride
She was so proud
She looked into my eyes, and she just smiled
I had never seen her so exuberant
I was happy because she was happy
She said no one can eat or drink in her car
She was so excited that she only drove it twenty-five-miles-an-hour
Scared that she would dent it, I guess
She parked far away from others
Not wanting anyone to hit her car
So when she pulled up to church
Everyone was looking to see who was driving this
Big blue Cadillac
She glided out of the seat
Opened the door
And the gazes
She had on her best outfit
She said, "Come on kids"
We looked at each other
Mocked her
Said, "Good morning" to other parishioners
We giggled
It wasn't until I was older that she explained
That car meant the world to her because
When she was a maid, the people she worked for drove a Cadillac
For her to be able to save her money
Years later to walk into a car dealership
Be treated with dignity
And drive off the lot with a Cadillac
She said it was faith that she had to one day have it
She said because of faith it let her know that just having the belief
She could have whatever she wanted
When she was approved for that car

She parked it outside of her house
The house that was directly across the street
From the people she was a maid for
She said, "Remember this:
This is a testament that if you believe in yourself,
You can have your dreams come true."

Eight Years

I was happy
I always wanted to have a baby
Even as a child I had my dolls lined up across the bed
They all had names, and I carried one on my hip
Played doctor on them
Rocked them to sleep
As I grew older and my siblings had kids
They were my living babies
I held them tight
Changed their diapers and fed them
So when the doctor looked into my eyes
"I am so sorry to tell you that you're not going to have any babies"
I thought about all the blood I'd shed
I thought about the tumors that kept growing and coming back
I was so quick to sign off to have surgery after surgery
The last surgery was my fate
I came home, and I cried
I have a womb, but I didn't feel whole
I no longer bled and that signified my womanhood
My breasts were no longer tender
I didn't break out with a pimple
So I lived my life and I didn't want to hold another baby
Until recently, babies started smiling at me
Children kept walking up to me
My heart started melting
So on the chilly morning when I woke up
Something wasn't right
With fear, I went into the restroom
It's been eight years!
I looked down, and I saw the blood
I shook
I went to the doctor, and there is a chance in a million
Your lining has grown back
I cried tears of joy

"The number 8 in the Bible represents a new beginning, meaning a new order or creation, and man's true 'born again' event when he is resurrected from the dead into eternal life." (The Bible Study Site)

New beginnings

Second chance

Doors opening

It took eight years

I Cried For You

The tears ran down my face
There is so much going on
I would pick up the phone and try to dial your number
It's been so long, I can't remember the number anymore
The receiver held in my hand
I held it to my chest
You're gone
I think about the times I would call
Hearing your voice answer
I wouldn't have to say a word
You would listen and say "Baby, is that you?"
I would tell you about my day
Dates that I had
Situations that I was experiencing
Your advice would be so simple
Voice always calming to my spirit
I can't call you anymore
I fill my days with busy work
Now I need to call you
My world is crumbling around me
I feel all alone
I want to hear you
I gather myself nightly
Surround myself with pillows
The tears soak my pillow
I tell myself it will be okay
Time will heal wounds
If I could just feel your arms
Hear your voice
I awake and the feeling is still there
I made a dish that you always made
It comforted me for the moment
I rampage through the garage
Found the box I was looking for
There it is...

Your answering machine
I bring it into the house and plug it in
I hear your voice
I start the conversation
I press play again
You say "Hello"
I say "Mommy"!

Promises Are Meant To Be Broken

I promise with all my heart
I promise to love you until the day I die
I promise that I will never leave you
Those were the words you spoke
I believed you

Promise me you're telling the truth
The reply is I promise
Promise that you will finish what you started
I promise

Promise me you won't tell a soul
Swear to me that you promise that we will go Saturday
Girl, I promise
Stop playing

We are going to buy that big house
Travel the world
Never have to work again
We laugh
You say "I am serious"
I look into your eyes
You stroke the hair away from my face
You say "I promise"

So when you leave
No words were spoken
There were no goodbyes
Reality hit
Promises were meant to be broken

I Want To Hurt You

My heart is shattered into pieces
There are no more tears to cry
I am angry
I want to hurt you
I want you to feel the pain that I feel
I did not deserve the treatment you served me with
I loved you
I wanted to have your babies
I wanted to lie in bed with you forever
I wanted to walk down the aisle
I wanted to be your wife
You hurt me
I want to hurt you back
I want to not answer when you call
I want to walk down the street, recognize you
And when closer, pretend I don't know you
I want to forget you
I want to sing the song "Bust Your Windows" by Jazmine Sullivan
I want the gratification of knowing that you hurt
Just as much as I do
I want to hurt you

Forgiveness

My lips quiver
I have prayed over it
I have read my bible
I have kept the secrets for years
My pain is buried deep down in my soul

You have lived your life
You have no idea
I am a prisoner of the circumstance
In order to be free, I have to forgive you

I take out my tablet
I write a letter to you
I start and the words won't come
I start again, and the pen writes the first word "I"
I stop

I have to do this for myself
It's been years
I can't take it to my grave
I have to release it

The memories flood my brain
I start crying
It feels like it was yesterday
I have to gather the strength

I look in the mirror, and I have aged
The gray in my crown is from the image I see
I go back into the room
I pick up the tablet again
This time the words begin
Slowly the pen glides across the paper

When I am done, the papers are many
I have emptied out every emotion that was bottled up

I forgive you

You can no longer hurt me

You can no longer keep me in the past

A strong breeze comes through the window

A smile comes across my face

I am finally free as a bird

I forgive you

After I realized that I had to forgive me

Roots

Deep in the South
There was a sharecropper
She raised her family by herself
They picked cotton
There were stories of moonshine
A young boy told tales of wearing overalls and no shoes
He said, "That's the reason why he's flat foot."
He said he had seen a lot in his days
Never talked about the bad
He said he grew up and he got married
They moved up North
Had babies, lots of them
He told stories of drinking, gambling, and he said he was real good at it
Working in the factory everyone looked the same
That was until they showered and the shoot came off
Then you realized that you worked next to men who were Polish, Italian and Black
I loved listening to him tell his stories
He being so much older I asked, "Were you a slave"?
He chuckled and said, "No"
It was important for me to learn my history.
Grandmamma was a sharecropper.
You can't be what someone tells you, if you don't know where you're from.
You got to know your roots.

Advice To My Daughters

I sit down across from her as she prepared to move into her first apartment.

I feel this is the best time to share with her what was instilled in the women in our family.

Lula Belle had seven girls and one son.

She died at a young age, so her girls had to become the women of the house.

Some had already moved out, gotten married, and had children of their own.

They took jobs in factories, domestic workers, and nurse's aides.

My child is looking at me, why I am telling her this?

I said, "Just listen."

Lula Belle's girls were very smart.

They had businesses: one owned an auto repair shop, another owned a group home, and others were investing in properties.

The girls had children, instilled in each a foundation in the church, and that there are ministers, bishops and elders within the family.

She is looking puzzled, and I smile

The sisters endured challenges, and they had a bond that couldn't be broken.

Their children grew up together and were each other's best friends.

Finally, looking at me as though she was ready to walk away

I explained that these women are my aunts and mother. That they built in each a foundation that whatever the world put before you, to always put God first.

These women didn't know what "No" meant! They were in male-dominated roles as an ordained minister, owner of an auto repair shop, and they weren't afraid to work for what it took for their families. They weren't quitters.

Some of the women had been married more than once, and the lesson is never being in something to say you're married if you are not being treated with respect.

My child is starting to realize what I am doing.

I had to explain that your parents aren't always going to be here

You come from a long line of strong women

If a man should ever raise his hand to hit her, don't be afraid to leave!

Going out into the world can be scary.

There will be sacrifices that she might have to make.

That she has support from her family

There are a lot of times young women feel that once they leave the nest if something happens, they have no one to back them up or come to the rescue.

A family unit never turns its back on one of their own.

I explained that she would have to learn to be creative with planning a meal, because if money ever gets tight you need to know the staples to fix. I've seen the women in the family put something on the table to feed their families. I said black-eye peas, rice, and ham hocks will feed the family for pennies any day. When our conversation was over, you could see the confidence had increased Shoulders up, back straight, and looking into my eyes, she got it.

Lula Bell's girls were survivors, and they passed it on to their kids.

We have passed it onto them.

This was the best advice I could give

The Womb

We all have a purpose
As a woman, it is my choice to want to have kids
I always wanted a baby all of my own
Time slipped away, and I missed my window
Fibroids filled the space where the baby was to be
Though they were removed, they always grew back
Holding babies, I still felt a flutter
The day the doctor told me that I would not have kids
I cried myself to sleep
I accepted my fate and never thought again about it
Until I sat across from the doctor
She was explaining something was wrong
Something was wrong with MY womb!
My eyes welled up
It's been so long
I have kept up with all my appointments
Had all my tests
What are you talking about?
She held my hand and she said we need to do more tests
Your womb might have cancer
As a woman, you know you have two breasts, ovaries, and a womb
Why would someone play this trick on me?
I can't even think about it
I can't fathom the thoughts that I will lose my womb
The doctor said we will do everything possible
Don't worry
Easy for you to say
I want my womb
I don't want cancer
I want to go back in time
When I was in love
When he and I made love
I want the seed to grow
I want to feel it grow within my womb
I want to birth the baby

I want to hold him in my arms
I want to know that my womb served its purpose
Some won't understand
I always wanted my baby
I cannot now lose my womb

If I Had Wings I Could Fly

Being in total bliss
Feeling like I can soar
Not concerned about anything
Stopped worrying about what others think
Standing up for myself
I look in the mirror and I am in love
With Me!
Not forgetting what struggles I overcame
No more tea and popcorn for dinner
No more wondering if I can make it
I made it!
Down on my knees I pray
Trusting that all will be alright
I take the time to smell the roses
I see the twinkle of each star
No longer rushing to get to nowhere
There is pep in my step
So when he sees me, smiles and says hello
I return the smile and say hello back
The conversations lasts for hours
I feel myself floating
"If I had wings I could fly, so let me contemplate"

Another One Bites The Dust

Fate wouldn't have it any other way
We meet at the coffee shop
Exchange phone numbers
Talk later for hours
We are hitting it off
He is everything I want
And I am the same for him
There are long drives along the coast
Convertible down
Wind blowing in my hair
Long walks along the beach
Romantic dinners by candlelight
The cute text messages
The look of love in our eyes

The first kiss is magical
We never want to leave each other
Our bodies blend and become as one
This is what love is
Until his wife returns from her trip

The Stage Is Set

You are driving down the dark road alone
You are not speeding
You see headlights fast approaching
Your heartbeat is racing
The lights flash
You wonder if it's for you
You weren't speeding
You pull over
As he approaches your car and asks for your license and registration
You oblige, but you get the courage to ask "What did I do?"
You have on a suit
Your briefcase is in the passenger seat
You feel that you can explain that it's a dark road and you know you weren't speeding
Your door is flung open
You are pulled out
He says, "Are you resisting arrest"?
You look bewildered
Handcuffs are snapped on your wrists so fast, like Houdini
How is this happening and how it is happening to you?
"Officer, I wasn't speeding!" you exclaim with fear in your voice
As he puts you in the back of the squad car
Another police car approaches
You hear them talking
Your car is going to be left on the side of the road
They figured it wasn't your car anyway
He gets back into the car and drives you to the precinct
Your charge is resisting arrest
When going through your things for booking, there is your briefcase
They look up and ask what you do.
That's when you look them in the eyes
You reply, "I'm the new Assistant District Attorney for the state"
The irony, they only saw the color of your skin
You were innocent
The stage has been set
Scene closed

Momma Used To Say

Growing up
I would stay in the shadows
People would forget that I was present
I would listen to the grown folks talking
My momma would be giving words of advice
Grown daughters and sons would return home for the holidays
Sit around the kitchen table
Talking about life
Experiences that they encountered
Momma would listen
Then she would start by letting them know if she agreed
If she didn't, the words would flow
How she would have handled it differently
Sayings like "kill them with kindness"
"You will be remembered for how you handled it" and not by a negative action
that they expected
She gave advice on what relationships should be
"Always respect each other
When there is no respect, the love has left the relationship
Remember that and move along"
She would wake us with a song or say it at the end of a phone conversation, the
words are engraved in our memories
"I love you, a bushel and a peck, and a hug around the neck"
As we grew older we call each other and remember those words
Sometimes we mimic her and say, "Remember what Momma used to say"

Hold On

You feel like giving up
Everything is slipping through your fingertips
Hold On
All your friends are busy
Don't have time to talk
You feel all alone
Hold On
Your loved one has walked out the door
Or they scream that they are done
Hold On
Work has you going crazy
Long hours and nothing to show for it
Hold On
Just stop
Take a deep breath in
Exhale
Though it might hurt now
The pain will ease with time…Just hold on!

Move

Ever feel like running away?
You know that you can't
So you picture where you would go
What the house would look like
It's by the water
Up on a hill
A view to see the sunrise
Just you and your babe
Everything is peaceful
No drama
The new street that you live on
Everyone is friendly
There is no animosity
There is just peace
You are able to sit on the balcony and paint
Paint the world that is filled with love and joy
You are able to walk around the house and there is space
Space that you can fill with words
Words of encouragement
Words of empowerment
The move didn't cost you thousands
It was free and you can move anytime you want to go
Just close your eyes and move

INTERLUDE

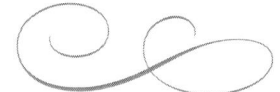

The Beginning

Growing up in Waterbury, Connecticut, the youngest of a blended family of thirteen children, I knew I was special. There was never a time that I didn't feel my parents didn't love me, protect me, and weren't my best friends. From the time I was a toddler and my parents were working class, I was taken care of by my aunts, brothers, and sisters until my parents arrived home. The highlight I fondly remember was being picked up from kindergarten by my father. In the doorway, I would see this tall caramel-colored man with his hat tilted to the side of his head, after he got off work. I would run into his arms and he'd lift me and give me a kiss. Beaming with happiness, I felt like I was six feet tall like him, and couldn't wait to tell him about my day. That was the beginning of our journey where I would go for rides with my father across the state, talking about life and listening to his stories.

My mother was twenty-one years younger than my father, and her personality was just bubbling with love. She would take in strangers and feed them. After working at a facility and seeing how they treated the foster adults, she became a foster mother. She spent the checks she received for taking care of the four women on dressing them like the rest of our family. There was never any difference. We were a family that included Louise, Helen, Gladys, and Jacqueline. At five years old, I was introduced to my first foster sister, and the word *foster* was never used again.

Faith was very instrumental in my parents' lives, especially my mother's. She had gone through many trials and tribulations and knew that it was nobody but God. As she became more active in the church, she went from missionary to evangelist, then fought to become an elder. During that time, women weren't thought of as preachers and especially if they'd married twice; it was frowned upon. While a freshman in high school, I was able to witness my mother being ordained as a pastor. She was the first African American female to deliver the invocation at a veteran's observance in our town. She strived to reach her goals and studied to earn more certificates. She wanted to be taken seriously and there were those who didn't want a woman in their pulpits. Watching her from the background, she was teaching me how to survive life's struggles with faith.

When she was disappointed and hurt by the treatment she received, she held her head high and didn't let anyone know she was hurt until she came home. Any obstacle placed in front of her, she found another way to get around it. I grew up feeling like the world was mine and didn't know what challenges were, because I always accomplished what I wanted from modeling school, president of school clubs, and jobs. It would later lead to my demise because when I didn't place in pageants, barely graduated from college due to a grade, or received my first unfavorable review at work, I didn't know how to handle it.

What I loved about my father was every morning and evening before he climbed into and out of bed, he was on his knees praying. If you happened to not knock on the door and walked in, you would hear him *having a talk with Jesus,* as the older saints explained. You knew not to interrupt, but I would stand there and listen and wonder would I ever have that type of faith. He had a large book, a bible study guide, that he was always reading. Between reading and having dialogue with my mother about the sermons preached at church, I was amazed at how much they knew.

My father and I would talk while sitting watching television, and he was puzzled at how many answers I knew on the game shows. Yet when looking at my report card, it didn't reflect my knowledge. He challenged me and I was blessed to show him before he died that I could be on the honor roll in high school, graduate college, and, though I'd left Connecticut, was able to tell him I had a job where I would be able to take care of myself and my mother. As he was transitioning to leave this earth, he didn't have to worry.

So between the two of my parents, I knew from my mother that when in doubt—pray; you don't know what to do—pray; and when all else fails—pray. She prayed for everyone: for their marriage, sickness, and if they were in trouble, she would pray. My father—on the other hand—always said, "Work hard, don't pay to be liked. Because when you stop paying and no one pays for you, they were never your friends, but users." And, "Ladies don't be out late at night, because the only things you will see are dogs and prostitutes." Two opposite extremes, and I didn't know at the time that all the wisdom they were sharing I would see for myself later in life. That faith is what you need to make it through any struggles in life.

PART 2

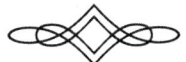

Daddy's Girl

The saying is when a girl is born
She is the apple of her daddy's eye
She is a Daddy's girl
My father explained that when I was born, that was the proudest moment
He was sixty years old and didn't imagine another child
But to see a little baby girl looking back at him, he just smiled
Talking to other men, they explained to me it didn't matter the age, having a girl is special for a man
He was my protector
He was the first man to ever tell me that he loved me
I was a Daddy's girl
We had father-daughter dates where he took me to Howard Johnson's to eat
This was our time
I told him everything from school, my friends, and any problems I had
He would tell me about growing up, jokes, and his embellished stories
I was a Daddy's girl
There were proms, debutante balls, and graduations and the glimmer in his eyes
Let me know that I was his legacy
I would finish where he never dreamed of going
I was an extension of him
The pride welled up in me to the point I felt untouchable
As I grew into a woman and began dating, it became difficult
He had raised the bar so high
He didn't ever want me to settle

He wanted someone for me that would treat me with respect
Love me with all their heart
Provide for me to not want for anything else
He died before giving me the honor of walking me down the aisle
Giving me away to my future husband
I am a Daddy's girl
As I look in the mirror, I see his eyes looking back at me
I look at my hands and they resemble his to the bend of the thumb
I know I made him proud

Bus Stop

Life is like a bus stop
You get on expecting to get to your destination
But there are stops along the way
You need to do due diligence to make sure you are on the right route
Knowing the right fare to get you there
Bus Stop
There are times that you need help and might require a transfer

It's not always a straight line
You will meet people along the way
Some will prefer not to speak
Others will be the social butterflies
Just remember it's a bus stop and they are passing through

Not A Day Goes By

Not a day goes by that I don't think about you
When a situation comes up, I think what you would do
Birthdays have come and gone, and I wish you were here
I see a mother and daughter out, and I wish it was you and I
I smile and tell the daughter she is blessed to still have her mother
I take your birthday off as a personal holiday
I celebrate you wherever I am at
I make sure I order your favorites dishes
I sometimes will wear your favorite color
When I see an orchid, I purchase the prettiest one
I place it within view so I can remember you
The pain is supposed to ease as the years pass by
That's a lie, because my heart still hurts
I know that no one will ever replace you
Yet, when I see an elderly lady with a cane
I pay close attention
I go out of my way to assist her
If I attend church and a woman comes in with a large hat, I smile
I finally got up the nerve to sit in your seat
It's been ten years, and it feels right to carry on
I speak words of encouragement to those I see
I try so hard to keep in touch with your friends
We talk about you and what you used to do
The laughs we share
We all miss you
There are your recipes I try to remember
I try to make it just like you
I get sad when I can't pick up the phone to ask what your secret ingredient was
There are times when I put on some gospel music and mimic your happy dance
Boy, I sure do miss you
The holidays are approaching
Still can't put up the Christmas tree
The last one was the year you got sick
It was up, the gifts were around it and I had to bring them to the hospital
It took me close to a month to take it down

I hid the tree

Christmas was your favorite holiday because all your children and grandchildren came home

You would start making your famous dishes the week before the holiday

You decorated the house so festive

You got all the gifts on our list and added an extra for good measure

You made us all feel so special

I put on your robe

Curl up by the fireplace and look at the flames

I wipe away each tear as they continue to come

A Mother's Love

The sacrifices you make
Bodies get distorted carrying a life inside
Birthing a child into the world
Teaching the child the skills to survive
Nurturing
Loving
Unconditional love
A mother will go without to ensure her child has
She is your best friend, your confidant, and more your mother
No matter how old you get, she is still your mother
She reminds you at each stage of your life, in case you forgot
She is the event planner for your birthday parties, starting at the first
She attends all your school functions
She is the chauffeur to all your events
She is the doctor when you're sick
A Mother's Love never ends
When you fall, she is there to pick you up
Doesn't end when you grow up
Her undying love never ceases
When she is gone
She is at peace

Gone

Like the wind that brought you in
You left
No goodbyes
No argument
Just …
Gone
The chapter didn't conclude
There was no happy ending
There was no riding into the sunset
Did it mean nothing to you?
Were they all lies?
You're just gone
After the first few days
Of worrying whether you were alive or dead
After coming to grips that it was over
I knew it was for the best
I accepted the times
I changed the codes to my heart
Opened the windows and let the breeze in
If you love someone you set them free
I thank you for my freedom
Goodbye

The Answer

There is a knock at the door
He appears to be everything that I want
Tall, dark and handsome
About six foot three
As he enters into my castle
A kiss is planted upon my cheek
I smell the scent of cologne
That intrigues me
We talk about the future
We talk about our goals
We talk about where this can possibly go

It's now about quarter past three
You let me know that you would never hurt me
That I am the only one that you want to be with
I tell you my concerns
And you explain to me that I am the woman you have been waiting for…That I
am the answer to your dreams

LET GO

Dreaming of a brighter future
Not in this tangled web
There has been pain, hurt, and deceit
Can't talk to my friends
They will say you should have left a long time ago
I tried
He would always find me
He would call around to the family
Someone would slip, not knowing
Let Go
There is a child who was bullied
Scared to tell the teachers
Scared to tell their parents
Scared to tell their friends
They didn't know where to turn
Let Go
There is so much going on
Too much to handle
Not enough hours in the day for all the demands
Pulled in every direction
Married to the job
Let Go

It's Hard Being A Girl

Wanting to be treated as an equal, even as a kid

Let's see who can run the fastest

No, I don't fight like a girl

So if I like to climb trees

Wear high-top sneakers and overalls, I am considered a tomboy?

Really?

Why can't I just be a girl?

There are those who are really good in sports

Those who excel in academics

Little girls have dreams of going to the moon

Running their own businesses

Even being the president

It's hard being a girl

No matter what we do, there is an excuse as to why we made it

"She must have slept to the top"

No!

In the workplace her voice is sometimes muffled

No one hears her ideas

Someone of the male persuasion can repeat it and get the credit

There are no tears because they will think you're weak

So we have to be extra smart

Extra fast

And do the job twice as good

No one said it would be easy

But, damn it's hard being a girl

Romeo and Juliet

Some get caught up in the romance of the forbidden love
Having a long list of what he or she should be
Discriminate if they show up in a different package
Come from a different background, race, ethnicity
What is love?
It is pure and it doesn't have any classification
Height or weight requirement
Color of your skin
It shouldn't makes you feel ashamed to let others know you're falling in love
Don't let others influence you of what your heart desires
You never know who they will be
Your heart knows when it feels
When you kiss, it will feel as though you explode
As you stand on one side
And he on the other
Forbidden by walls
Remember love conquers all
O Romeo, Romeo, wherefore art thou Romeo?
(Martin, 1996)

Turn Back The Hands of Time

I am standing on the edge

Looking out at the land

The land where you farmed

The land where you broke your back to make a way

I look at your hands that are rugged, swollen, and show the scars

You never gave up because you said you wanted a better life for us

There was never an alarm clock to wake you

You didn't complain about going to work because it was what you had to do

You talked about the amount of cotton you picked from sun up to sun down

You told the stories that your hands were raw until they bled

As I rode down the highways

Looking at the fields of cotton

My eyes welled up

I asked to stop the car

I got out and I breathed the air

I can only imagine

You shared the tales of having to drop out of school so that you could work the fields

I stretch out my hands now

Though they resemble yours, they have never worked in the field

My hands are smooth like a city girl

If I could turn back the hands of time

I would let you be the childhood boy

Experience the things that you missed growing up

I would let you go to school

You would be an architect

You always liked building things

I understand that I can't

That was the road that you had to travel

The journey wasn't always sweet

But if I could! I would! Turn back the hands of time

Up North

There are plenty of jobs
There are opportunities for everyone
You can make it there, you can make it anywhere
You left your family
You said you would send for them
You would go first
Share a room with a stranger
Until you can stand on your own
Working sixteen hours shifts
Sweat dripping from your brow
You worked to make a new life
You worked in the factory
You worked anywhere you could
You were leaving the past behind
You were going
Up North
Everyone was migrating to the place where they said the rich lived
They needed someone to drive their cars
They needed someone to take care of their houses
They needed someone to care for their children
There were days you missed your own, but you knew that soon it would be over
There were hardships
There were times you couldn't go to the same places others went
There were times that you could only enter through the back entrance
You made it work
You kept the faith
You knew that it was better here
You had to believe that because there was no going back
You sent for your siblings
You sent for your spouse
You sent for your children
Together you lived in one house
Up North

Dreams Do Come True

When I was a small child I believed that
If I worked hard I could accomplish anything
It was engraved into my being
So I listened to my parents share their stories of their childhood
I took nothing for granted
As I got older, when I took my first trip out of the states and shared the pictures
with my parents, I saw a sparkle in their eyes
It was no longer a dream coming true for myself, but for them
I enjoyed calling them and telling them about places I'd seen, people I'd met, and
foods I'd experienced
I always wanted to have my very own house
Others said it couldn't be done
I scraped and sacrificed
To hang their pictures on my wall made it bittersweet
I planted the rosebushes, her favorite flowers
She was able to see them bloom before she passed
I place her engagement ring on my ring finger
His watch on my wrist
The world is my canvas
I intend to paint
Crossing each item off my bucket list
I wrote just for them
I can hear them in a whisper
Saying "Where next?"
I look to the skies and reply

There Something About You

There is something about you that I can't shake
Maybe it's the way that you look at me with those brown eyes
Maybe it's the deep baritone voice that says "Hello Sunshine"
I don't know
When I come into your strong embrace and you pull me closer
I inhale the smell of your cologne
Dolce & Gabbana, the one arouses my senses
Or maybe it's the way that you kiss me soft
There is something about you that makes me want you more
As I caress your hands and feel secure
There is warmth that comes over me
When you ask how was my day
I know you care
When you ask if I want cream in my coffee
When I am cold, you gently place the covers over me not to wake
There is something about you
When I stand from afar and admire you
Commanding the room with your presence
You catch me looking
You smile those pearly white teeth at me
Making me feel like a school girl with a crush
When I arrive home from work
And you remove each item of clothing
Massaging each limb
Erasing all stress from the day
The bath water is ran
Rose petals tossed in
You take my hand and guide me into my oasis
As I bathe
Eric Benet softly playing "Chocolate Legs"
There is something about you
That makes me thankful that you're mine

Like an Onion

Slowly peeling back the layers
Trust issues
Past relationships
Hurt
Broken promises
Abuse
Each layer coming off
Self esteem issues
Walls protecting my heart
Lack of communication
Another layer is taken off
Until I am bare
Vulnerable
Sweet at the core
Exposed
I look at you for acceptance
You're crying

Learning to Love Again

You're so patient
Like an abused animal
I am afraid of your touch
For fear that I will be hurt
We talk for hours
Slowly I am letting you in
We start as friends
You say you want nothing more
As the days pass into weeks
Weeks turn into months
I realize that I am starting to feel something
I look forward to seeing you
Our hands intertwined as we walk
Under the mistletoe, you ask for a kiss
You say that you love me
I look into your eyes
And I say I love you, too

The First Meeting

We have talked on the phone
Decided on a location
Anticipation
Will he be everything that he said?
Will I be what he's looking for?
Pictures have been texted to each other
Appearance is acceptable
I changed six times just to find the right outfit
He has showered, cologne splashed just right
Not overpowering
Slacks, dress shirt, shoes shined to perfection
You let him know you will have a red flower right behind your right ear
You agreed on the time and place
And as you approach the hostess
She says you're expected and escorts you to the table
As I am walking to him, he smiles
That smile can light up a room
My nerves subside
He stands and pulls out my chair
I exhale as I take my seat
We talk
Order our meal
And laugh about the stories we share
The restaurant is closing
We don't want the evening to end
He asks, "Have you ever met your soul mate?"
I blink my eyes as if he just read my mind
I respond "I think I just did"

24 Hours

Suitcases packed
Running away
He makes me feel like the world is complete
He says that he needs me
So I typed the letter
I quit
Gave the landlord notice
Tickets arrive by courier
I got twenty-four hours to be with him
Friends think I am crazy
Well crazy in love is what I will be
No one understands
Let me explain
I am the air that he breathes
I am his rib
I am the light in a dark world
I am food that he eats
When he is thirsty, I quench his thirst
People search their lifetime for the meaning of love
When it is in front of them, they pass it by
He lets me know that I am the apple of his eye
If the world ends tomorrow, he wants me in it
I got twenty-four hours to live in it

How Deep Is Your Love?

The question was asked
Is it deep enough to hold my heart in it?
Can I open my arms wide enough to hold you?
Will I drown in the overflow of your love?
How deep is your love?
Will you shield me from harm?
Will you comfort me when I am sad?
Will you humor me with laughter?
Will you keep me warm when the world is so cold?
How deep is your love?
I really want to know
You turn to me and say
Will you provide shelter from the storm?
Will you build me back up when I am torn?
When tears fall from my eyes, will you be there to wipe them all away?
Will you promise to let me in and not push me away?

My Gift To You

I sealed it in an envelope
Placed it in on your pillow
It's my gift to you
Take good care of it
And open it later when you're alone
Later that evening you open the envelope
You have waited for this moment
You unfold the paper gently
Press out the creases
It's symbolic of our love
It's a picture of my heart
I love you and I always will
Take good care of my love
It's my gift to you

With This Ring

We are gathered here today
To join this man and this woman together
With this ring
They stand before God
Announcing their love for one another
There has been hurt and pain that they had to overcome
There were challenges that they had to endure
The road wasn't always easy
Their love blossomed like a flower
Seeds were planted into soil
It was watered with tears
The love between them shined so bright
When they realized that nothing or no one could separate them
To live each day as man and wife
Partners in this journey we call life
Until death do they part?
With this ring

INTERLUDE

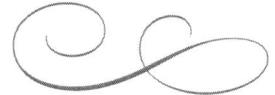

The Journey

Leaving the nest is what every parent prepares their child to do. They have poured wisdom into you. They want you to know right from wrong. Their wish always wants the best for you. Being the head of the household, your father always wanting to protect you from harm. The role of a mother is to nurture her child, always wanting you to be close. I couldn't wait to leave for college and anticipated the day when I would have my first apartment. I thought that I knew everything, and yet, I was so naïve.

I was away from home for the first time, living in Virginia. I was calling home daily to give reports of everything that I was experiencing for the first time. As I met more people, the calls were less frequent.

It wasn't until my sophomore year that I realized I didn't know as much as I thought I did. I had met the cute fraternity boy and we went on a date. He didn't have a car, so it was okay that I drove. We went to a friend's apartment. I recognized one of the guys sitting on the couch. We sat and watched television and I thought this was a perfect date. He asked me to follow him into one of the bedrooms so that we could talk. We sat upon the bed and we chatted for a few. He moved in closer and he told me he thought I was beautiful. We started to kiss and it moved fast from there. Teenagers away from their parents, hormones rising, and two consenting adults is how it started.

That was until he pulled out a gun and pressed it up to my temple. He proceeded to bite me on my nipples, stomach, and my mind drifted to another place. The question in the back of my head is how he could do this if he thought I was beautiful. It got late and it was time to leave. I drove back to the dormitory and cried myself to sleep. Ashamed of my actions because I thought he liked me.

A mother's love is never ending and can sense when something is wrong. The next morning she called and I answered the phone. I heard her voice and the tears began to roll. I told her everything that happened. I never heard the phone drop. My father picked up the receiver and heard the rest until I stopped. Anger ran through him, but I was too ashamed to know he was on the phone line. My father handed the phone back to my mother who was left to console.

In the background a call was being made to my brothers to come to Virginia to handle the situation. The irony was that I was scared for my family because I didn't want them to be harmed or to get into any trouble, and yet for the rapist I also wanted to protect.

My mother got off the phone to calm my father and cease the bounty. I rang my girlfriend to tell a fraternity brother what had happened, that my family was on their way, and that I didn't want this to get out.

That incident happened over thirty years ago, and I still felt that it was brought on because of my appearance. I proceeded to gain weight to cover the shell. My trust in men had changed because the first man who ever loved me never hurt me and why would I expect the same from another man. When I had let my guard down and believed that this was the one man who could show me love, something always happened.

There were men who came into my life that I loved with all my heart over the years. One man after another disappointed me for specific reasons. I found some had wandering eyes, cheated on me with my best friend while I was away at school, or I found out that they said all the right things, but their actions spoke another.

My wall went up to protect my heart and my new love became my job. I strived to be the best at whatever position I had. The people at my job were my friends, my family, and my child that I never had.

There was something still that I felt missing, and it was on a trip to California that I felt my calling. I came back to tell my elderly parents that I was leaving, and it was my father who looked in my eyes and said, "I won't always be here." Something in his tone let me know that it was the right decision because I needed to become independent. I had family in California, so I had support. Within two months I had given notice at my job, packed two suitcases, sold my belongings and had a one-way ticket to California.

I knew no one except my family, and I slowly began to venture out to the unknown. I was working sometimes two jobs to make ends meet. Because I couldn't go back to Connecticut. Because I didn't want to fail.

My father's health was declining and I would come back annually to see him. I had so much excitement to see him that I would just lie on the covers next to him. Just listening to him breathe and feeling protected from the storm.

I remember like it was yesterday I came home after he had surgery. It was snowing and I went outside to shovel the snow. Being that I was the youngest, a girl, and my parents always paid a neighborhood kid to do this. Well the kids had all grown up and moved out of the neighborhood. I never had done this task of shoveling. Something that my father had done for years and made it seem like the snow was as light as a feather. He sat and watched me and I struggled, but he stayed in the window from afar. It felt like the muscles within my chest had exploded and

I was in so much pain, but I couldn't let my parents down. I thought I had done a good job. While I was inside recovering from the ordeal, my father had changed clothes and slipped outside. Shovel in his hands and as the man of the house—no matter if he had a hole in his side, wasn't to lift anything, and was supposed to be recuperating—he was still going to be the man and complete the task.

When I saw what he was doing, I lost it because of the fear he would injure himself. We got into the biggest argument. I was leaving the next day and we were still mad at each other. I kissed him goodbye and sat on the shuttle crying all the way to the airport. It was something within my being that knew that it was the last time I would see him. I wanted to become the protector and do everything in my power to show him I could be strong, I could provide, and I was the woman he raised me to be. He, being the proud African American patriarch of the family, not wanting to be seen weak, even in the months before his death wanting to be remembered as strong.

Within months he was in hospice, my mother had called to tell me to come home, arrangements were made. I spoke to him and he could barely whisper into the phone. I said, "Daddy, I love you. I got a new job paying me good. I will be able to take care of Mommy, it's okay if you want to go. I was to leave on a Thursday morning and at 6:30 a.m. Wednesday while getting ready for work my mother called to tell me his condition. She placed me on hold because another call was coming in. She came back on the line, and I could tell by her tone something was wrong. I said, "Mommy, what's wrong" and she said, "They said he's expired." She had to get off the phone and go to be with the man she called Honey. She had to see him before he was gone.

I sat naked on the bed, called my sister who lived close by, and said, "Daddy's gone." She rushed to my apartment and there I sat in shock. She helped me get dressed, she hugged me while I wept, and she took control of my life for the next seventy-two hours. She placed calls to get me home immediately, few words came out of my mouth, and she took time away from her family to bring me home.

It was a blur from that point on while preparing for the funeral, making sure my queen was taken care of, and my king was laid to rest.

My father died eight days before my birthday and we laid him to rest on St. Patrick's Day, aka, St.Patty's Day. As I delivered his eulogy, I recited all the accolades about this man we all loved. The question that I proposed to the group was "Who will have my back now"? The minister, from the podium, answered "God will always have my back."

As we drove to his final resting place, my brothers, nephews, and grandnephews came to hug me, each whispering in my ear that they would always have my back. The tears flowed, and my father was lowered into the ground as I said my final goodbye.

When I left Connecticut, I had a small box of his belongings that I put away in my closet to open after my birthday. When I opened it, I found his Timex watch and placed it on my wrist and it started ticking. My heart skipped a beat and I had to catch my breath. I felt he was with me at that moment, and I knew whenever I had a situation that came up to remember that he had poured into me that I wasn't ever alone and that I was a Saunders.

I found myself excelling at work, meeting new people, and enjoying my life again. The opportunities were opening up at work, and I was getting promotion after promotion. I had friends I was meeting that I was spending time with, and I found I was spending more time with them than my family. My time consisted of work, church, and going out with my staff.

It was at one outing that I met Jamie and we hit it off. He had me laughing, talking, and feeling I could let my guard down. He was the complexion of dark chocolate, a beautiful smile, and he was confident in his demeanor.

We went out a couple of times before he invited me to his place. I felt comfortable, he was the ying to my yang, and those kisses sent me over the moon.

On this particular evening something was off. He invited me over and didn't greet me at the door but instructed me to come into his apartment a different way. The lights were off. He was standing in the dark and came over to greet me with a passionate kiss. Clothing coming off, guiding me to the bed, and we were going to make love, I thought. Instead I was seeing someone I didn't recognize. He was aggressive, forceful, and hurting me. As I expressed my displeasure, it only angered him more. He didn't stop and I tried to free myself. He was stronger than I had imagined, and I was pinned to the bed until he was finished. I gathered my things and dressed in the bathroom where I wiped blood from my private spot. As I came out of the bathroom I looked at him, and he didn't look at me nor acknowledge my presence. I left through the front door and got to my car where I called my niece crying. As she calmed me down so I could drive, she wanted to know where I was so that she and her boyfriend could pay Jamie a visit. Again, here I was protecting someone who'd hurt me.

I remember going to my primary doctor the next day to be examined and her asking questions of my injuries. I explained what had happened and she wanted to get the authorities involved. From fear of it being exposed, I begged her not to: "Just complete the examination and run tests to make sure that I'm okay."

Three years later, I would be at a football party with my girlfriends, focused on having a good time. Not looking to meet anyone, because my luck thus far, while in California was not the best with men.

He stood on the side of the dance floor holding a drink up to his lips, his light brown eyes following me around. My friends had to point out that I had an admirer. This time I had became more confident, and as I danced closer to where he was standing, I said hello. I got off the floor and introduced myself to the mysterious man. We danced, conversed about the game, and made a bet if the team I picked won, I would not have to give him my phone number. I lost the bet and numbers were exchanged.

We dated for months and there were still unanswered questions. We were intimate more than a few times, and one time is all it took. I was late and scared to tell anyone my period was missing. My sister urged me to take a home pregnancy test. I brought one home and before I could finish urinating on the stick, it was changing colors: confirmation there was a child.

I had a new job, I was not married, and I had a man in my life that was still a question mark. I called him to come over and explained our predicament, and Rod said whatever I wanted to do was fine with him. This was supposed to be a joyous occasion, yet I was sad. All the things I wanted to happen in my life weren't happening. I wanted to fall in love, get married, have a house with a white picket fence, and then start a family. It wasn't supposed to happen like this.

I had to figure out what I wanted to do that would be best for me. I made calls to my sisters and my mother. My mother voiced her concerns saying, God doesn't make any mistakes but I was supposed to be married. One sister said have the baby and she would raise it for me. Another sister encouraged me and said she would help me. One other sister shared her decision to end a pregnancy when she was younger. It wasn't the right time, she wasn't ready to become a mother. There was still time later. I met with my doctor and tests were ran to officially confirm that I was pregnant. When asked my decision, I said I wanted to end the pregnancy.

The appointment was made and I needed to take time off from work. The other conversation came from who I least expected it from. I had started a new job where I had more responsibilities; my female boss was very demanding, and I never saw her smile.

There was this one night that I was still at work preparing for my time off and making sure that nothing would go amiss while I was away. My boss was still in her office working when she came out and started making small talk. She asked what I was going to do while I was off. If I was going anywhere or doing anything special, and there was something different in her demeanor. She was softer, seemed human and interested in me. I took the chance and let her know what I was really going to do.

She confided in me and shared her story as well of once being pregnant. She said she had made her decision based on the man she was pregnant by. That it was a mistake, and that she loved him but wasn't in love with him. Very young like me, she said not to put guilt on myself. She said I would find that special someone later in life. I had just started to excel within my career, and it was the right decision.

Friday morning, Rod was to come to my home and drive me to the appointment. As the time was growing closer, I was becoming nervous. I kept calling and getting voicemail. He wasn't coming and I didn't have enough time to have someone else drive me. So I got in my car and drove to my appointment. He knew the address where I was going, so there was still hope. I also called my sister and explained what happened and where the doctor's office was.

As I was being prepared for the procedure, the tears ran down my cheeks. The nurse held my hand and the doctor asked again if I wanted to go through with it. I nodded my head and they began. When it was over I dressed, feeling like I had made the worst mistake that I couldn't take back. I'd have to live with it for the rest of my life.

The nurse came in and said, "Someone is here to take you home." I was hopeful it was Rod with the light brown eyes.

My sister walked into the room, her arms flung open. She took me into her arms and said, "You will be alright."

I drove myself home; my sister rode with her with her two young daughters following me home. She undressed me and prepared me for bed. That night she stayed with me with her three daughters. Holding me in her arms, all three of her children lying across my bed, and my phone never rang.

It was seven years later that I would be at the bank, annoyed because there was a customer holding up the line. I was on my lunch break and needed to hurry, make a deposit and still have a quick bite to eat.

This customer had on a courier's uniform, and was flirting with the teller while she was busy with his transaction and flirting back. It wasn't until he was finished and turned around that our eyes locked onto each other. It was Rod, and I looked through him like I didn't see him. He kept walking and turned around as if he remembered where he recognized me from. I turned and looked at him as if I had no clue.

I put the wall back up to protect my heart. I had lost something each time I let the wall come down, and the last price I paid was too much.

PART 3

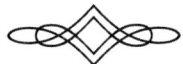

Take The Hint

When he starts questioning you
Where have you been?
Why aren't you responding back when I text you?
Take the hint
It's one thing to start a relationship
Get to know the person
Meet their friends
Meet their family
When there are secrets
They always will come to light
Warped speed relationships start and end the same way
Take your time
If he tries to get to all bases before you know his last name
Run like a pit-bull is after you
Deep in your gut you know
If you would just take the first hint

I Would Have Freed More If They Only Knew

Looking into the eyes of my sisters

I see fear

I see that they have given up

Running away wasn't an option

They were determined to stay

Take the abuse

Take the punishment

I see her and I nod my head in acknowledgement

Signaling that it's okay to leave

You don't have to stay

I have seen the makeup trying to cover the bruises

I have heard you thrown up against the walls

You might have tried to muffle the sound

I heard each one out loud

As you rush to work, dropping off the kids, and making sure your secret is kept

I noticed that during lunch you are sitting in your car, never with a bite to eat

Enjoying your solitude, I wonder where you are

My sister, you don't have to endure this pain

I have an escape all planned out

You say that you love him

You can't leave him

That I don't understand

That he's only being a man

I look at you with disbelief

I do understand more than you know

I received the call the next day that they found you

You got your wings

Gone too soon

He's locked up

The kids are in the system

There was another way if you would have seen that you were free

---

You Can't Control A Free Spirit

She met him and he seemed to be saying all of the right things
People always gravitated to her so it seemed only natural
She didn't let anything dim her light
She was focused
She loved life
As she got to know him more, it seemed like they shared common interests
Going to the concerts to hear music
She said she could float on each note
Seeing plays where her imagination could run free
Being at the beach and seeing a sunset
She was comfortable in her own skin
So when he started making comments that she looked good, but she would look
better if she lost a couple pounds
When she went out with her friends and he texted her to ask where she was at
She didn't think much of it, he must be concerned
When he started showing up unexpected at her job
Calling throughout the day asking what she was doing
She started feeling uncomfortable
She decided to confront him about his actions
He explained that he loved her, cared for her, and didn't want anything to happen
to her
He said when she wasn't around, he worried about her
She looked him in his eyes and said, "I have luck on my side
I am free as a bird
I am not to be caged
My spirit guides me in the right direction
When something doesn't feel right my spirit knows"
And by his actions, she said
"You have to go"

You Can Wake Me

I love it when you are in love
You're giddy
You can't wait to come home to be around each other
Just watching TV
Knowing that he's in my space
Makes me smile
Getting those cute messages throughout the day
Letting each other know that we are thinking about them
Planning secret rendezvous
Keeping the spice in the relationship
Cooking special meals for each other
Seeing something special while you're out shopping and surprising the other
It's the balance that we each bring into our union
The love between each other that you do what you have to do to make it work
So when I am sound asleep with a couple more hours before I have to rise
I hear him trying to not wake me
I don't get upset
Instead I throw the covers off
The left leg is out just enough to catch his attention
The one I know that he likes to feel shake while upon his shoulder
I smile when I feel him getting back into the bed
He snuggles very close
A kiss is placed so gently on my shoulder
He knows that I am not asleep
I turn to him
I love this man so
I whisper in his ear as I roll on top
You can have me morning, noon, or night
Baby, all you have to do is wake me

Where Would I Be?

Lord, I fall on my knees
I give you thanks for keeping me
I am thankful for you providing shelter for me
I remember I had no job
No money to move to another place
No funds to pay a mover
Scared I would be on the streets
Family telling me that they had no room
Not even for me to sleep on their floor
There was that one person who took a chance
There was that one person who loaned me money to move
I thought about having diamonds and furs
Not even having five dollars in my wallet
I remember eating popcorn and drinking iced tea
I remember robbing Peter to pay Paul
Each step of the way you had a special person holding my hand
I wanted to give up and call it quits
You never gave up on me
I think about the call that came
I hadn't posted for a job
I didn't tell anyone I was looking
Each step of the way doors kept opening
To everyone's amazement
Slowly restoring what I had lost
Always right there
There were times that I questioned where you were
When you showed up, you showed out
Lord, I thank you
Because I remember
Where would I be?

Time

As I age
The body is getting slower
The mind is a terrible thing to waste
The clock is ticking
I look in the mirror and I see the gray appearing in my crown
My vision isn't the same as it was
The pep that was in my step is slowly becoming a burden
Traveling the world was always a dream
Money in the bank
Seeing my heirs prosper
What would my legacy be?
I look at my hands as they glide across the paper
They don't look like mine
The clock will eventually stop
Don't know when
Time…

Glory

A change is going to come
If only you believe
No more war
No more hate
GLORY
I will see you
You will see me
No color barriers
No walls
We will walk together
Same mission
Peace
Love
GLORY

Be Somebody

I don't care what you want to be

Just be the best

Thinking there isn't anyone to care

That you have to settle

Be the father to your child

Be the mother to that little girl

Use your mind to excel

Don't let them tell you no

Be somebody!

Road blocks will come

That's expected

It's the will to continue that makes you stand out

Be somebody!

Do You Know What You Want?

Standing in the shadows
Unaware that time is passing you by
You say you want to be loved
When it is there, do you know?
Have you set up barriers that prevent you from seeing?
You want to be successful
Is your mind closed to the possibility of being outside of the box?
You want to live in the glass house
Are there stones around it?
Travel to exotic places such as Dubai, Greece, or Zimbabwe
Do you have your passport?
As the little girl looking in the mirror imagining that she conquers the world
Don't forget that dream
Don't get older and let them slip through your fingertips
When asked what you want
Proudly stand there
Knowing in your heart what it is
Conquer the world
As the little boy who is told he can't
Show the world you can
For it starts with you
So we ask you again
Do you know what you want?
The answer is yes

Goodbye To The Past

No longer a prisoner to the past
There were good times that far outweigh the bad
Kissed the boys and made them cry
Friendships that went through the seasons
Lovers that were there to share a moment
Tears that were shed enough to fill an ocean
Standing outside in the cold
So that I could not feel the burning inside
There were enemies that ate at my table
Drank my wine
Letting go of the baggage
Some were there for the ride
Taking a piece of me with them
I say goodbye
There were material things that I gave away
Not to have bondage of the price you paid
New beginnings
Meeting new people
Can't have the past present
They want to hold me back
Want to be the crab in the barrel
Want to tell me about the past
Want to hurt me
Saying goodbye
The saying goes people come into your life for a reason, a season, or a lifetime
It's the lesson that they bring
Knowing the difference
A reminder of who I used to be
Not recognizing that I have changed
Not wanting to look back
Moving forward
I hug you, tell you I love you and say good bye to my past

A Shot Rings Out

As I walk down the street
A shot rings out
A scream is heard
Another life is lost
A mother's child is gone
There are protests
Black Lives Matter
Blue Lives Matter
All Lives Matter
All I know is a child is gone
A gun is in the wrong hands
Someone didn't value a life
Someone walked into a sacred place
Took aim at the saints
One by one their souls escaped
A shot rings out
Everyone is running
Someone is trampled
Someone just wants to go to the club with their friends
Someone just wanted to walk down the street
Someone just wanted to make it home
A Shot Rings Out!!!!

Momma's Nightgown

There hanging in the back of the closet
A reminder of her
I can still envision her walking down the hall
With her gold slippers and that nightgown
Coming home to see her, I would snuggle up in her bed
Laughing, telling her all about my adventures
Holding her oh so tight
Feeling that flannel gown against my skin
Falling asleep staring at her
It's been years since she has passed
Sometimes I go to the closet and just press it against my cheek
Feeling alone and no one to talk to
I will shower, put on baby powder, and slip into
Momma's nightgown
As I climb into my bed, I feel comfort
I sleep like a baby and all the troubles are gone until I awake
The anniversary of her passing is coming up
I call my sisters, I find that I start crying, telling them how much I miss her
Silence is on the other end of the receiver
Finally I stop and I can hear
She is crying, too
Each tells me that they took a nightgown from her house
Have it hidden in their drawers
When it's cold or they are sick, the gown comes on
We find ourselves chuckling
Wondering what she would think
I say it's her way from heaven to let us know she is there always
Momma's nightgown

Close Your Eyes

Close your eyes and make a wish
As I do I am thinking what I really want
I want to see my parents again
I want to say I am sorry to my first love
Let's start all over again
I want my father to walk me down the aisle
I want my Momma, sitting in the front row with her purple fancy gown on
I want to say I do
Carry baby Allen to full term
Live by the ocean
See the sunsets
I want to feel you come up behind me
Giggle in my ear
The warmth of your body
Makes me secure again
Every year as I get older
I want to turn back the clock
To the time that we first met
I want to keep my eyes closed
And make a wish

My Letter To Theo

Dear Beloved,

I remember when we first met. There was electricity in the room shooting between us.

There was something special that I can't explain to another.

I was curious about who you were and you the same. We exchanged numbers and talked until the wee hours.

There was the party where we had our first dance. Your friends were jealous and told me you belonged to another. I slipped away into the darkness, not to appear until years later.

I invited you to my home that was blessed that day as a celebration. You came late, but you came. We sat on the couch like teenagers. Nervous, stealing looks at each other, and the sparks were there. It was months later that you came again, candles burning throughout the house to guide our steps. The first kiss was magical, something was awakened within me. I was yours from that moment on. The love we made was like we were in our own secret garden.

Our first Christmas we exchanged gifts and I never questioned why it was two days early. Something within me knew that there was a lie brewing within.

Weeks became months, and months became years, the same schedule. The knock upon the door, the excitement of waking to find you standing there, my arms opened to let you come in. Each time I dressed in my new Cache bra and panties set from Lane Bryant, scents of perfume sprayed between my breasts, behind my ears, and my knees.

Daily calls, texts messages and the pictures. Lord, the pictures were sent back and forth. I was falling in love with you. She called me once and I didn't pick up. I listened to the voice mail message and I stood there knowing that you belonged to her and I had to let you go.

I craved you until I found another lover, told you to never call again, and that I would be okay. I lied and within months you called when I needed a friend. I had lost my mother, lost everything, and was ashamed. Your voice was always so assuring that it calmed my nerves. You said that you needed to see me and I was to pick you up at a secret location. I brought you to my temporary spot. You looked around and I felt ashamed. You said it was okay, and you wanted to help me get settled. As I got my self-esteem back up from being broken, you always spoke encouragement. I would pass ideas by you and like a chess master, you guided me through each move.

Soon I let you back into my heart, my bed, and my head.

You were the air that I breathed and without you I felt incomplete. I'd rather have a piece of you than to have you not here with me. So the visits began again every week. A knock on my door, I would wake up from sound asleep, feeling like a kid waiting for Santa. I would rush to the door.

I would lie next to you in my bed, telling you about the places I traveled, the sights that I had seen, and wishing that once you would steal away just to be with me. Always with excuses, you hoped I would understand.

Year after year the stories continued, and my heart couldn't take anymore. I gave you an ultimatum and you ended it with me.

That didn't last long, within a week you were back with me. We talked about having kids, but that never happened. You never wanted to get married and that was my desire. There were special occasions that I wished you would attend. You showed up at one, but you had to leave.

My sister pulled me aside and asked what was I doing? You're wasting your life away with a man who can't be with you is what she explained. Something stuck and I placed it on the back burner. It wasn't until I saw you that last Tuesday that I knew it was over.

You walked into the house, kissed me on my lips, we made love and I looked into your eyes. I saw my life flash before me. There were holidays, birthdays, weekends that I could never get back. You went into the bathroom to shower and wash me off of you. This time I went into my shower and I washed you off, too.

I stripped the bed and threw on some Beyonce on Pandora. You dressed and left, and my body didn't miss you.

It was strange but I left the following week, no phone calls, no text messages and no pictures please. I focused on myself. I was turning my life around. I didn't think of you once and my freedom was found.

When I returned I went to Macy's before it closed and laid upon the new mattress. I explained my story to the saleswoman who patted my hand and told me it was okay. She did me a favor and had it to be delivered on Tuesday.

I don't hate you, but love you for all the memories you gave. There were grey skies that you made blue, there were times that nobody was there to hold me, but then there was you. There were times that I wanted to quit and you told me I wasn't a quitter. There were tears that were shed and you wiped away from my eyes.

Theo, I thank you for unlocking my heart from the box that you held for years. I took a leap of faith and floated away. If I ever see you again, I hope you will understand because of you I now know what I want in a man. Thank you for loving me. Thank you for making me laugh. Thank you telling me I was beautiful when I had forgotten that I am.

Love,

Me

Don't Forget

Don't ever forget
You are beautiful
You are created in God's image
Don't ever forget
Your complexion doesn't define you
Don't let anyone tell you
Your lips are too full
Your eyes are too big
Baby, look in the mirror
You are beautiful
Don't forget
When you think you are not smart enough
Jobs are being passed by
Baby, make a list
And find you another job
You are smart
Sometimes too smart for your own spirit
But don't forget that you're enough
When they try to break you
Tell you that you're nothing
Remember that you're something
When they talk behind your back
Remember that they see the star that you are
Don't forget
Strive to be anything that you want to be
The only thing stopping you
Is when you…
Forget

Exclamation Point

I am screaming to the top of my lungs
I am not invisible
I matter, too
I can see you looking
Don't be afraid of me, too
See me for who I am
Not define me by the color of my skin
I am standing here
Not going anywhere
Demanding my place
Exclamation Point!

Appreciate My Thickness

A Nubian Queen
Built like no other
Thick hips
A little jiggle in my walk
No silicone in my rear
It's all real
Many pay for the gift God blessed a sistah with
No silicone
When I come into a room
Take a pose
I know what they are looking at
Wishing for my thickness
I am proud of the blessing that my ancestors
Have bestowed on me
Know my history
Know that many would have paid top dollars for me
Breeding is what I was supposed to do
You think it's cute now
I walk with my crown because I know
I know what my fellow sistahs had to go through
Appreciate my thickness!
Birthing princes and princesses
I appreciate my body
Stretch marks my medal of honor
My King loves me
Kissing my chocolate full lips
Turns me around to see my reflection in the window
Head held high
Crown tilted a little to the side
I appreciate each curve and my thickness

He Will Restore

My faith was tested
I never thought it would happen to me
Losing everything
Asking Him to supply my needs
Not thinking I had to experience
Everything to appreciate what I had
Questioning Him and everyone else
Seeing people who were supposed to be friends leave
Finances gone
House gone
Friends gone
Family gone
Lord, what else is there to take?
I found myself talking to you more
I found myself on my knees more
I found myself going to church more
Realizing that what you wanted was to get my attention
When I humbled myself before you
Forgetting what my needs were
You started blessing me
Better than what I had asked for
I had wants
But you gave me what I needed
You restored my harvest
The seeds that I had planted along the way
Helping another
Keeping my relationship with you
Investing in my community with my time
Forgiving those who hurt me
My faith restored
He will restore

Weak In The Knees

Baby, you make me weak in the knees
I received the text message
Telling me everything that you want to do to me
My mind went to that place
I took an early lunch
Drove my car straight to you
You hear my car come to a complete stop
Knowing that you are watching me
I slowly strut to the front door
As I walked into the house
You greet me with kisses on my lips, neck and ear
I moan from the heat that is rising within me
I bite my bottom lip
Legs feeling weak with desire
Clothes come off in the foyer
You lift me up like I am light as a feather
Carrying me up the flight of stairs
Feels likes it took forever to get to our bedroom
Telling me how much you love me
Telling me how you couldn't wait for me to come home
That you desire me
That you can't wait to taste me
Make love to me
Like synchronized dancers we coordinate each other's moves to a perfect beat
It can't be any better than this
We're newlyweds. We just don't know that it's been seven years because we love
each other more each day
My legs shake like an aftershock

BABY MOMMA

I had dreams for her
I wanted her to be different than the rest
He started coming around
I didn't like him
He had bad intentions, I could feel it
Months later her stomach was growing
Hiding the facts from me
Found out on Facebook
Never thought that I would become my mother
Acting the very same way she did when she learned of her daughter's fate
I cried when I called and got the words confirmed
What about my dreams?
You're going to be a baby momma
Can he provide for you?
Are you going to be married?
Questions were thrown at her worse than darts
No answers could be good enough

The baby was born
We all helped out
Where's the daddy?
He moved on to the next
She's seven months pregnant
As he calls to tell you
The tears well up in your eyes
I stand in the doorway listening
Each tear is a dagger to my heart
I never wanted you to be just a
Baby momma
One by one, dreams became a reality
As the father started his new family
We've seen less of him
You're going to be alright
Make me proud
Baby Momma

Don't get upset
Stay focused
Take care of your baby
Get that education
Get that paper
If it didn't work out the way you plan
Don't trip
You're a baby momma
Something not everyone gets

Feed Me

I am hungry for the Word
I found that as I was lost
Not knowing where to turn
I forgot something that was important
You are the bread of life
I want to be saved
I want to have eternal life
I want to be caught up in the rapture
Lord, feed me

Strawberries And Cream

After being abused by many
I didn't know how to appreciate a good one
My walls were up
Let me hurt you before you hurt me
So when God sent him
I thought he made a mistake
Wrong address
He didn't get frightened of my cold walls
He smiled and I started to defrost
He called when he said he would
Flowers were sent to my door
Romantic dinners would make Casanova look bad
Walks along the beach
Sunday morning church services
Slowly the walls were tumbling down
Not wanting to be physical until I was ready
He said he just wants to show me how much he loves me
He kisses me softly on my forehead
Plays love songs on his guitar
That he wrote just for me
Writes me poetry
Reads me sonnets
As he proceeds to feed me strawberries and cream

Please Me

If I could tell you
I am too ashamed of what I have done
He said if you would just "please me"
God, what else can I do?
He said in your shame you stopped praying
In your time away from me, I became jealous
Who else was taking up your time?
I said, "Well I like to sleep late"
He asked, "Would you like to sleep forever?"
"No!"
I said, "Well I like to hang out with my friends"
And he replied, "There is no greater love
than he can provide"
He said, "Please Me"
I looked confused
He said, "Feed your brothers
Clothe those who need to be clothed
Take care of those in need"
I said, "Well I am not rich"
He said, "It's not money that I want
I want you to please me
I want you to worship me
Praise me
Fellowship with your family
Show those who are lost the way to me
I already have forgiven you for your sins
All I ask of you, please me"
"I got it!"

INTERLUDE

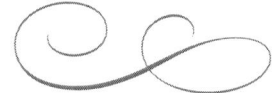

The Test

I had prepared for my father to pass. I knew he was much older than my mother, so it would eventually happen. What I didn't expect was: nine years later she would leave me.

At an early age I knew more than most children about preparing for death. I knew the definitions of wills, power of attorney, and irreversible wills. Walking around in fear that my parents who were older than most would leave me at any moment.

Grieving for a mother who's passed is worse than losing a father. I don't know if it has to do with the birth canal. I don't know if it is feeding from her breasts. All I know is that I wanted to die on December 30, 2006.

My mother was my best friend; she was always there since I was a kid when my friends would back out of events, and she was always there. She was always at pageants, volleyball games, and graduations. That's what she did and never complained. Working jobs in the factory to cooking in restaurants, getting her hustle on selling furniture, we never went without. She led by example: that you should always have your own money as a woman.

I remember as a kid listening to a pastor at a church say sex was beautiful. I wanted a definition of what sex was. She explained it to me as best she could. I was only six years old. She said, "You keep your panties up."

As a kid I remember being molested in the closet at my cousin's house. I remember my mother trying to shield me from the effect as best she could. The damage was already done. I was damaged as far as I was concerned.

I was curious about sex as a kid and always wanted to know what it was all about. I wanted to know what was beautiful. I can recollect as a child receiving a birthday gift from one of my sisters, a lingerie set that I wore thinking I was a grown woman. I would talk on my white princess phone from Southern New England Telephone to the cute boy in class.

My mother was not only a woman of the cloth, she was my mother. She was one that I could talk to up to a certain degree. Since I was a kid until I was in my late thirties, she was the one who I could always depend on.

The test happened in 2004 that changed my life forever. I loved my mother with all my heart and with the daily hustle of work, my calls were less frequent. Instead of daily it became once or twice a week that we would have our calls to talk. Her birthday was approaching in June, and I wanted to surprise her. I decided I was going to send her a ticket to visit the majority of her children living in California. She was so excited that she started packing her suitcase weeks before.

She was in her seventies and was taking medication for ailments such as high blood pressure, congestive heart failure, and others. So she always told us about her daily fourteen pills she had to take. It was part of the routine, and we even teased her. On one of the calls, she also had mentioned that at church during choir rehearsal another member refused to sit next to her and complained that she smelled. She was upset about it and voiced her concern to the choir director. My mother was one who always bathed, dressed to the nines and took pride in her appearance, so though she mentioned it, we didn't take it seriously. She also mentioned her weekly visits to McDonald's to get her two cheeseburgers, french fries and diet coke soda. This time she said she had paid and then drove through the drive-thru without getting her food until she was almost home and then turned around.

The day came for her arrival at San Francisco International Airport. I got off work early to pick her up, and there was something that was different. She walked slower, and though she had a cane it was as if she was walking on ice. We drove out to my home, and she got settled as I kept a watchful eye on her. Her behavior was alarming, and I contacted my sisters so they could also be observant. I felt she was overmedicating, and I gently brought up the subject with her because I wanted to know if she needed help. She said she was fine, and she wasn't taking her medication more than needed.

My brother drove from Manteca, California to pick her up to have her spend time with his family. It was two o'clock in the morning when my mother awoke and started packing her belongings. She told my brother she was going on a bus. She didn't remember being in California, his home, and this was the beginning of the mystery. He made calls to all of us for help and was crying on the other end of the receiver. Her visit with the grandchildren was cut short, and he was bringing her back to my house.

Seeing my mother in a dazed state, we made calls to our sisters back on the east coast. My mother was going through something. We didn't know what to do, but we were getting help. Glenda, my sister, was flying from Atlanta to meet my mother when she changed planes in New York. The other sister was calling from Maryland to speak to my mother's primary doctor to make an appointment the following week. Once they returned from New York, my sister Glenda was at my mother's apartment the following morning when she noticed that instead of pouring sugar into her cup of coffee my mother was pouring it on the kitchen table. Glenda acted quickly and rushed my mother to the emergency room.

There was a piece of the puzzle that Glenda knew that the rest of the family wasn't aware of. My mother had been involved in a car accident. She was hit from behind by a retired police officer and had hit her head. She didn't seek any medical care and had told Glenda about it. She said she had felt fine and didn't want to get him in trouble.

At the emergency room, my mother was examined, the on-call neurologist was called in to examine her as well, and tests were being run. There were x-rays, CAT Scans and an MRI and the results were in. The wind beneath our wings had left us as he uttered the words "She has fluid on her brain, we'll need to do surgery, and also she has dementia. She won't ever be able to live by herself," And now Glenda has to repeat those words to each of us.

My mother underwent the surgery with flying colors but would be in the hospital the next two months. Each of her kids took time off from work, flying to Connecticut to be with our Queen, staying at the hospital round the clock until we couldn't keep our eyes open. We would drive to her small apartment and collapse across her bed until the alarm went off to start our shift again. Meeting with doctors, being her advocate, and making sure she was comfortable.

We made arrangements and had my mother come to California to live with four of her six children. I was the power of attorney and made doctor appointments, coordinated between siblings, and tried to figure out our next steps. She lived with my eldest sibling for a month until the day my sister came home early to find the caregiver left a half hour early and my mother was going to attempt to get the mail where she could have fallen. It scared my sister and we decided it was best to find a group home for her that had twenty-four hour care and specialized in dementia.

For two years we took her to church, all types of activities, had family gatherings and we were still in denial. We knew she would never be the same as she was, we were going to still let her have her dignity, but we didn't understand the disease. We found adult day care for her to still be active, a facility where she was seen three times a week. If they noticed anything, we were alerted.

A change we noticed was she never wore fingernail polish in the forty plus years she was my mother. But, I picked her up one day and she had bright red polish on her nails and she loved it. Her new routine was she wanted her nails and toes polished and we adapted because it made her happy. She had a phone in her room to talk to us—her friends and family—on the east coast and that brightened her days. She knew something was different and wondered why she had to live there, why she didn't have access to her checkbook, or wasn't able to drive any longer.

I surprised her and took her back to Connecticut to visit our church home and they escorted her to the pulpit. My stomach was in knots because "what if they asked her to speak, what if she had an episode, and what if she didn't remember." Being protective I didn't want her visit to be an embarrassment and only wanted to make her happy. She got on the microphone and when she spoke the person I remembered from my childhood was back! We were standing on our feet. I was in amazement, tears streaming down my face, and family members hugging me because she was going to be alright. While on this visit, she demanded to see her stepchildren and two out of three came and she held their hands. She told them she loved them. She seemed childlike and again I was puzzled because she hadn't had contact with either before she became sick. So again, I thought it was the dementia. I still—to this day—felt she knew it was her last visit.

The year was 2005 and was special because she was going to turn seventy-nine years old this year. I sent for my sister Glenda to come out from Atlanta for her birthday. I had my sister Tara bring Glenda, and I brought my mother to church. The moment was priceless because I wanted to make my mother's last years her best. Seeing my mother's expression, her crying tears of joy and being that it happened in church made me feel I had done one of my jobs as her daughter.

The next year with my mother were times spent that I couldn't trade if I wanted. We spent time talking, going for rides, and my accepting her where she was in her life. I accepted the roles had reversed and became that the child I never had, the one that I didn't birth, the one I didn't spoil was looking across the table at me. My mother was my baby. I thought about her daily, with each passing moment, and if there was an outfit that I thought she would love—I bought it. If I knew she would love to go for her favorite dish of fried shrimp—then we were off on an excursion for her to eat and be happy.

It was at a family meeting with her primary doctor that explained to the family she had Alzheimer's. She explained the expectation of decline: if she wanted her favorite cheesecake to let her have cheesecake, and I didn't hear anything else. My sister heard that it's normally not the disease that the person dies from, but complications from the body shutting down. It was as if someone said it, but again it didn't register because I just remember nodding my head. She had long term memory loss. When she stumbled with the words, we would help her, and we didn't understand what that would mean in stages.

She was declining and we were so focused on her other health issues that it slipped past us. When she had a stroke in September of 2006, was moved to a convalescent home, and her breathing became labored, we concentrated on her being healthy.

Early in December we rushed her to the hospital because she needed oxygen to walk from her bed to the restroom. Tests were run for the flu and pneumonia, and a specialist was called in because she was getting worse. We were told she was coming home, and then the results came back. The news hit us like a brick wall. She had lung disease and was going to die within days. Spending Christmas in the hospital, she said it was the best Christmas she ever had.

She was moved to another room where they administered comfort care, and we gathered. Family members coming to say goodbye, singing spiritual hymns, and reading the bible to her as we held a vigil around her bed. She was so happy and we had to put on a mask that we were, too.

I can remember my bishop and pastors of the church coming. They met with us and reassured us of what to expect, comforted us with words of faith, and it was in the late hours that my pastor came back. He met with my brother separately and told him he would have to step into the role of the leader. My pastor stood at the end of my unconscious mother's bed and spoke to her. He saluted her: "Job well done."

At home, I went through the paperwork my mother had prepared years before she became ill. She had written out her obituary, menu of what to be served at her repast, and what she wanted to be buried in. It was like she knew that the responsibility had passed from the eldest to the youngest of her children; she didn't want there to be any confusion. She knew exactly what she wanted even when she was gone.

Everyone was going through their own feelings, going to their private places to heal before we could stand as a united front to the public as strong children of Reverend Betty L. Saunders.

During that time I went along with the motions, but the emotions were flooding me. I was lost. I had no one to get up to go check on, and I had no one to memorize their medical records. I had lost my father years earlier, but had prepared for it because he had cancer and was in hospice.

Losing my mother was unexpected, and I was losing it. I couldn't make myself get up and go into my home office and work. The consequence of not working meant that bills weren't being paid. The main bill was the mortgage.

The home that my mother had done a blessing over in front of my friends and family I was getting ready to lose. I was getting calls within a month, asking if I wanted to do a short sale within two months, and was afraid I was going to be foreclosed within three months.

It was during that time that I felt alone. I was the product of a blended family, yet the rock was gone. No one was coming forward and saying you did the best that you could. I was held responsible for caregiving for my mother and she was gone! Had I failed?

In the back of my mind I was thinking: *Could I have saved my Mother if I had moved her to another hospital? Was there something that I missed? Was I too naïve and trusting of the doctors?* I always wondered should I have gotten second and third opinions. My final thoughts were: *did they kill my mother and I let them do it?*

I didn't know how to communicate what I was feeling. I ordered my Mother's medical records and went through each page. I made copies and brought them to a former nurse who was a lawyer. There was guilt hovering over me, and I needed to know I had made the right decision.

During my research, I came upon an article about caregiving's aftermath that mirrored my feelings. After caring for her husband, Wayne, for four-and-a-half years, Sharon Vander Waal was going through a period of reflection. "You feel that somehow you should have been able to control the uncontrollable, which is illogical, not rational thinking, but you can't push it away," Ms. Vander Waal said. For her, faith was a refuge from those feelings, along with her insight that, "I'm just a weak vessel who tried to do what I could, but it was out of my hands." (Graham, 2013)

By March, 2007, I had acquired an attorney for advice after revealing to my family that I was broke. I hired a realtor to sell my home, and was wondering where I would end up.

Fear was creeping upon me; I had a few friends, who offered to pay my mortgage for a month, one sent a check for a couple of months payments. I was searching for a place to lay my head with no job. I was selling my personal possessions so I had gas in my car and food to eat.

The test of time came when I sold my place, found a job making less money, and borrowed money from the realtor so I could pay the movers.

I had to humble myself because I was the one who'd made six figures, traveled the world, had diamonds and furs. Here I was begging to have money to pay movers to move me from a 1700 square feet townhome in a gated community to an 800 square foot apartment.

Also, interesting things happened during this time. People who were along for the ride when I was making big bucks, paying for the drinks and dinners had disappeared. Just like my father had told me, but I was too dumb at the time to realize. I leaned more on my church family because I felt that my real family had shunned me. If you didn't have room for me to lay my head, suggested that I stay in a shelter when you had a three-bedroom home, there was something that I needed to learn from that.

I needed to lean on the person who was always there. I didn't know it at the time because I felt that God had left me also. He had let me down by letting my mother die. He let me down by letting me lose the house that she blessed. He had let me down by not saving me before I lost it all. My siblings, who were supposed to have my back, were on their own journeys. I had so many questions on the predicament I was in that I—a preacher's kid who knew better—was questioning GOD!

PART 4

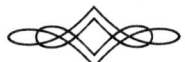

Touch Me

I am so cold

I can bite your head off if you attempt to come at me incorrect

I don't care

I don't have anything to lose

I have lost everything

So I walk into the church

Anger built up

I thought I came late enough so that I wouldn't have to touch you

There is a request and it is simple

Hug your neighbor

It is as though I have been slapped against the head

The person on the other side of receiving is needing me just as much as I need
them

This is the first touch and maybe the only touch for the day

So I grab them into my arms and I exhale

I hug them and they hug me, and it is something so euphoric

I felt it, and it was the beginning of my healing

I was touched

I was comforted

I was told that I was loved

And it was pure

Two strangers coming into the house of the Lord

Not revealing our wants

Just being in the presence of the Lord and letting him minister to each of us with just one
Touch

It Was Worth The Wait

Waiting on the promise that it would be restored
I have cried a many nights
Prayed so much
People came in and out of my life like a revolving door
Trying to trust again
Writing down my dreams
One by one
Slowly
Goals
Lists
Books like the *Secret*

Being Patient
As opportunities arise
Hoping this time would be it
Realizing finally I was on my deadline
Surrendered
The list shortened
Smiles are now my new normal
My faith has been restored

Sing Me A Lullaby

There is nothing better
Than being in love
Kisses like sunshine
On a dark day
Body heat to keep me warm
When I am cold
He likes to sing to me
He likes to look into my eyes
His voice is like a silky smooth baritone
I love this man
As he places me on his lap
Rocks me to sleep
Stroking my hair away from my face
My head lying on his chest
Hearing his heart beat
It's music to my ears
He sings me a lullaby, and I close my eyes and go to sleep

Spending Time With You

Every little girl needs her father in her life
He's the first man to tell her he loves her
He's the one she measures every man she meets to
So when he is gone, there is a void
Who is there to protect her?
Who is she going to tell her secrets to?
I can remember sitting on the front porch
And just being in his presence
Watching him read the paper
I would sit there and not say a word
Sometimes I would ponder questions
He would see the inquisitive look on my face
Asking about life
What does it mean?
Walking with him
He seemed like a giant to my small frame
I didn't mind looking up
I enjoyed spending time with him
Watching TV
Going for rides wandering around the state
Not knowing our destination
This was before GPS
Looking for something familiar to lead us back home
Eating dinner at our favorite spot
It was that time with him that was priceless
I thought that he would live forever
When he passed, though I was a grown woman
I was still his little girl
I was his daughter
He was my best friend
My father
The memories of spending time…
With you

He Speaks To Me

In my quiet space
He speaks to me
Telling me right from wrong
There are times that I want to do it on my own
Those are the times that I come back
And apologize because it didn't turn out right
Never angry
Forgives me over and over
I had to learn my lesson
He loves me unconditionally
More than I will ever know
Once I stopped running
Thanked him for not giving up on me
And I listened to my Heavenly Father from above

Knight In Shining Armor

Wants to be swept off my feet
Carry me away
Ride into the sunset
He's everything that I prayed for
Has the key to my heart
We will never part
Uphold my honor
This is real and not a fairytale
Accepting me for who I am
Not perfect is what I proclaim
We are two peas in a pod
People compare our love to
John and Jackie
Ossie and Ruby
He's my knight in shining armor
We are living happily ever after

The Will

A piece of paper
Instructions to be carried out
Dividing up assets
Heirlooms designated to your loved ones
Stating what to do with your remains
People fighting over a piece of paper
Greed separating families
Nothing is written about the feelings
The words that weren't shared
Some were left out
Sitting in your favorite chair
Trying to hold onto what is left
There is one thing you forgot
How do we go on without you?

74 Columbia Boulevard

The house has so many memories
You were so proud to purchase it on your own
The accomplishment was swept under a rug
You, a woman with an elementary school education
Overcoming obstacles
Working from being a domestic, factory worker, to entrepreneur
I remember being a little girl going with you to look at the house
We were the only ones of color on the street
This is the neighborhood you're quite familiar with
It houses doctors, lawyers, and professionals that didn't look like us
When you signed on the dotted line, you were setting an example for your young
daughters to follow
Each room was filled with l.o.v.e.
Decorated just the way you dreamed
Logs in the fireplace burning
Sitting watching your children
Our bellies full from the feast you prepared
Laughter filling the halls
Grandchildren running up and down the stairs
Hot summer days
Windows open
Family cookouts
Everyone coming together
Eating, dancing, and happy
Seeing you in your garden
Planting flowers
Your pride was to place your hydrangeas in vases throughout the house
Harvesting your vegetables for Sunday dinners
This house represented so much that we didn't see
As you pulled your car into the driveway
This was yours
People had doubted you
Told you that you were crazy
To live in this house, on this street, and being the only African American it would
never happen

You kept your eyes on your prize
You got the victory
When you climbed the stairs to your room
You said you were thankful for each one
As you walked down the hallway
Opening each bedroom door, looking at us as we slept you prayed for each one of your children
The road was not always easy
So when you rose every morning
Went into your kitchen
You said you loved to cook
You thought about the times you cleaned someone else's home
Cooked in someone else's kitchen
This house was yours
As you got older, it was too much
For you alone
You would sit at the window and look for your bird to visit… the robin
You called and told us that it was not the same
You and your next door neighbor had lost your husbands
You wanted to be close to your children
It was a hard decision
The sign went up
For Sale!
It will always be home
The memories etched in our hearts

Yesterday

I can remember like it was yesterday
It was Christmas Eve
You would be gone within six days
I am going to spend the night at the hospital
It's my turn to watch over you
We looked into each other's eyes
I knew you were leaving
No tears
I have to be strong
No words
Just listening to each other breathe
I held your hand
I had flashbacks of all of our times together
Mommy and daughter times
You taught me to be a lady
How can this be happening?
How can you leave?
My heart is breaking
I remember combing your hair
I remember you taking me to school
I remember you telling me about sex
I remember you sharing your stories of growing up
I remember you taking strangers in
I remember you always praying
I remember when you would take me shopping
You got your new hats
You were known for your hats
Put it on your head just right and made your entrance at church on Sundays
I remember talking to you on the phone daily
Hearing you laugh
That laugh I still try to mimic
I remember you always cooking
I remember watching you make your favorite dishes
Pineapple cakes, greens, baked macaroni and cheese, pork shoulder, and red
Kool-Aid

We called you for the recipes
It never turned out like yours
I remember laying my head on your chest
I knew I was too old for that
It was something about you, Mommy, that made it alright
I remember like it was yesterday
Your smile
Your smell
The way you feel

Guardian Angel

There comes a time in your life when you wonder
Who will be there for you?
When there is no place for you to turn
Someone will come forth
Out of the shadows to stand with you
Letting you know that you don't have to suffer alone
You really don't have to suffer
The guardian angel said, "If I have a sandwich, you can have half
If I have ten dollars, you have five dollars from that"
It's all about how you treat people
Don't judge a book by its cover
Think that you are too good to speak
It was the janitor that vouched for me
It was the maid who loaned her the money
It was those you thought were not worth your time
They were the ones that God had blessed with an extra blessing
They were the guardian angels
Listening to stories of how those who were living in glass houses were ashamed
when the glass broke
When you stop caring about what others think
Living your life for yourself
Not trying to compete with others
You never know how others are supporting themselves
When the doors had been shut
The guardian angel showed up
Opened a window
The story didn't end
Just a new chapter had begun

It's Raining

There is something about the smell of rain
Windows open
The smell of rain coming in
Hearing the raindrops hit the roof
Dancing as they hit the tiles
A cleansing is exactly what is needed
I awaken from sleep
Dress in my sweatpants and hoodie
Pajamas underneath
Pull on my rain boots
Umbrella by the door
Out in the rain
I am able to think
I can feel the rain hitting my face
Tiny splashes of cold water
Mixing between my warm salty tears
I love this time of year
When the rain comes
Nurturing the Mother Earth
Perfect to snuggle in the house
Watching the rain come down
Planning for all the things we are going to do
Candles ready
Wine ready
Warming massage oil
Baby, I love the rain
My mind is clear
I know exactly what I want
It's you
As we sit in the rain
Looking across from each other
Like a mime
Moving in sync
Soaking wet
Come inside my world

Dry off
Let me love you
Let's sit in the comfort of shelter
Enjoying each drop that appears
Watching the rain

With My Hands Up

I have never been a protester
I have stayed under the radar
Until today
Today I am the one with my hands up
Followed around the store
I have enough money in my wallet to pay the salary of the cashier following me
I am trying my best to stay in control
Not guilty until proven innocent
I know I haven't done anything except walked into the store
I realized that I had taken so much for granted
I am the only one in the store that looks like me
I notice that others are walking around the store
No one is being followed
Except…me
I am walking down the aisle when I hear his voice
"Did you find everything that you're looking for?"
"Well, yes I am quite aware of how to read
I can find my way around a store"
I notice backup is coming down the aisle
"I haven't done anything except walk in your store"
As my voice goes up because I know my rights
"I know that you're following me!"
Someone who you are thinking is guilty
Someone who just wanted to get an item for the holidays
While you are busy following me
Having staff zone in on me
There are five people walking out the door with merchandise!
As I protest treatment
"I demand to be treated as an equal
I demand to be treated as a human"

You have called for the local police
They speed to come
Black woman
Educated

Masters

Money

Nothing taken into consideration

You only see me as Black

Sorry that I came into this store

I am standing here with my hands up!

My Body Is Calling

I miss you
No, I am lying
I am craving you like an addict
I miss you
The mornings of calls to check on me
The text messages with the special pictures
To remind me of what I am missing
I miss standing in the door naked
The cool air hitting my nipples
I am missing you coming in
Hugging me
Kissing me
Your lips tasting like Listerine and Colgate toothpaste
Thinking about the night before
Your call telling me all clear

I was up waiting for you
Showering to smell like honeysuckle
Shaving so I was smooth
Spraying BeautiControl Relaxing Mist in the air
Candles burning
Lighting the house
Smells like jasmine
I am aroused
You lift me up into your arms
Carry me down the hallway
Lay me across the bed
And answer the call
My body is calling

I Smell Her

You keep telling me that I am the only one
This time you forgot the mouthwash
As you lie on top of me
Looking into my eyes
I smell her
I turn my head
Not wanting to kiss you
Feeling like Julia Roberts from *Pretty Woman*
We are making love without kissing
As we climaxed
There was never a kiss upon the lips
In the back of my mind
I think you're just a trick
I am the side chick
Only thing I didn't get paid

I got up afterwards
Showering the scent of you off
Stripping the sheets off the bed
No remnants of you
Just the faint smell of her in my nostrils

P.I.M.P.

Not what you imagine
I am not anything what she is
My self esteem is through the roof
I am believing what you told me
Until ...
You slipped
You never called me by her name
I was always baby
No way to confuse the two
I turned the tables
I let my heart become cold
I became the P.I.M.P.
There is no emotion
This is a job just satisfying our needs
It's all about me

What I need
What I want
If you can't deal
Let me go!
I am:
Pretty.
Intelligent.
Worth **M**illions.
And Ready to **P**lay.

Dear God

Are you listening?
I have laid in the bottom of the barrel
I have asked and nothing has been given
I have lost everything
My child, my family, and now I stand here
Asking, what else can I do?
I have been a good Christian
I thought I was
I was real busy, so I haven't been talking to you lately
Oh…when I needed you, I prayed
I forgot who you were when the times were good
I didn't stay in constant contact
My bad
I thought you loved me
Why would you let me experience such pain?

I have wanted to give up
I wanted to end it all
I wanted to just take a couple of pills
Followed by a chaser
I wanted to join those who I loved
I wanted to be at peace
I wanted to be humbled
Not suffer
Not be in pain
Not feel this thing I call a heart
I just want to be happy
I want to feel you protect me from harm
Restore everything that I lost
Unless you feel what I lost was a burden
Then reveal it to me so I understand
Please answer me

So I understand
I have prayed

I have stayed on my knees
I have fasted
I have talked to the elders
I can only come to you

Acceptance

I have got to accept you're gone
I have packed up your belongings
Delegated each item to your heirs
Nothing can bring you back
Recipes have been copied
Pictures shared
Acceptance that you're gone
It's not happening yet
I am still longing for you when I go to our places
Holding your bathrobe
Smelling your scent
My heart stops for a moment
I come across your journal
Seeing your signature
Your thought process in your sentences

I can read when you were happy
I can see when you were sad
You're gone
I have to accept it
I have to realize that I can't talk to you
I can't feel you
I can't hold you tight
You always had soft skin
I want to hold your hand
I want to look into those baby brown eyes

I want to hug you for the last time
Over again and again
Not letting go
I know I have to let you go
I know I have to believe you're in a better place
I have to have acceptance

It's 2 A.M.

It's two o'clock in the morning
Sleeping sound
Phone rings
I answer
I hear you
You want me
I say "It's 2 o'clock in the morning"
You know
You say you awoke yearning
You want to feel my skin next to yours
You want to be deep inside of me
You want to hear me moan your name
You say you need me
It's 2 A.M.

Curious

Out of curiosity I searched your name
It's been over twenty years
I don't know why I wanted to look back into my past
Maybe because it's the holidays
I am feeling lonely
Whatever

I typed your name into the search field
There you go
I see your picture
You have aged
Look happy

Then I scrolled through your pictures
I see a picture of your wife
There are pictures of your family
I see your friends that I remembered being around
It's at that moment the tears well up

Was this the life that I was supposed to have with you?
We were young
I remember the last time I saw you
We laughed
Talked about life
Dreams
We made love
You said you loved me
I later called you
You didn't answer
You could not come
When I needed you the most
The other woman that I saw you with
I remember her now
I knew she looked familiar

I had made a decision to leave you

I had a dream to pursue
You moved on
I thought I did, too

I wasn't supposed to look back
I opened Pandora's Box
The emotions flooded my essence

Give Me Strength

As I walk through the valley of death
Lord, I pray that you give me strength
So much is going on
Too many burdens to bear
I have traveled down the road
I came to a stop
Not knowing which way to go
When all my friends left
My family fell apart
I had to pray, Lord
Let me have a forgiving heart
There were times that I wanted to surrender
Thought it would be much easier
I knew you had a purpose
You hadn't shared with me my part

I have been weak with temptation
I know I have sinned
It was in these times that I felt alone
That you stepped right in
I had to look to you for my strength
There were times the doors were shut
I needed a push, a tug, and a nudge
To make it through
It's been a journey
There was a price
I thank you for giving me strength

A Brighter Day

Got to believe
That there will be a day
That's better than the one I am in
It can't get any worse
When you have given your all
They say it's not enough
Oh, there has got to be a brighter day
When I have worked until it feels my back has broke
When the rent is due, and I don't have but a nickel in my pocket
A message comes: to stay strong
There will be a brighter day
Don't give up

It's Back

I received the call that I have been dreading
She took a pause
She said, "Had you heard?"
A long silence
My response was "Tell me"
I held my breath
As the words came out of her mouth
Through the receiver that I held in my hand
I was thinking about how I hate the word cancer
I was thinking about how we had been counting
Five years is the magic number
Will the doctors see a spot?
Close to where it had been removed before
I am speechless
My heart stopped beating
I felt that the light had been turned off
I am sitting here
She says, "Are you there?"
I come back
Voice trembling
We got to pray
We got to stay focused
In the back of my mind I am thinking
Why has cancer been coming?
It's taken someone from me
Tried to scare me
I can't see the light at the end of the tunnel
I say we are going to be alright
I think I am saying it more for me than for her
I hang up the phone
I slide onto the floor
Into a fetal position
This time I feel different
Because it's back

He Won't Answer

I got weak
I called
Rehearsing what I would say
The phone rings
He is looking at the number
He recognizes it
He remembers the discussion
We said we had to move on
He remembers reaching out to me a couple of months
The pain is still there
I know better
I promised that I wouldn't go back
But I am weak
I need him
I need him to come and hold me
He won't answer

INTERLUDE

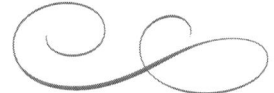

The Testimony

I received three cards from three different women with the words stating "This Too Shall Pass" inscribed in each. At the time I didn't see a way out. All I saw was I was drowning. I couldn't swim, and if I jumped, no one would catch me.

Slowly things were unfolding and being revealed. My mother was gone; she was in a better place, and I had to accept that I was still here on earth. I had to live. If not for myself, I had to be the example of what she intended me to be. She always said I was special and had a purpose.

The church was her sanctuary: she was very active from being at Sunday school, bible study, choir rehearsal and church service. I couldn't make myself go to where she found peace. I felt God had taken away everyone who I loved. The funny thing is: the church wouldn't let me go.

I don't know how members of the church had my phone number, but I had various members calling to check on me, telling me they loved me and were praying for me.

When I would enter the church, I wanted to sit in the seat where Mother always sat. I had a feeling that if I could feel her presence, it would help to heal the hole in my heart.

I felt that I was wearing a mask because here I was broke. Going from making a six-figures income to giving two dollars in the offering basket. I'd pinned a flier on the bulletin board of the sale of my house, hoping no one recognized that it belonged to me.

There were people coming into my life for a reason and I had to open my arms to receive what they were bringing. The first was my attorney who I felt was a father figure who guided me with my assets, directing my steps, and telling me that we were going to make it through.

There were female ministers who were praying for me, holding me, wiping away my tears. I had to share what I was going through because I needed help. Being a private person, it was difficult to share my experiences. A visiting minister named Dr. Wanda Turner was preaching a sermon in the pulpit, sharing how she had filed for bankruptcy. She'd lost her home and had the desire to want a home again. How she drove in neighborhoods where she wanted to purchase another home, found a home but needed an additional ten thousand dollars. She was praying for help because the bank wasn't going to give her any money. Her maid overheard her conversation, and it was the maid who gave her the money. The minister's testimony: it's how you treat people and don't judge a book by its cover. And, she was able to purchase a house again.

When I decided to sell my home before it was foreclosed, I knew of a realtor who lived in the community. I had to trust her with my story and what I planned to do. She gave me a book to read—*Secret*—that was the craze and had everyone talking.

It was her way of trying to reach me and helping me stay focused in the present, looking towards the future, and seeing that within myself I had the energy to come through.

She scheduled the Open House and the realtor who knocked on the door was a former employee from a job I had when I first moved to California. Within a week there was an offer to purchase the home. My wish had been to find a job before the offer came, because I wanted to keep the house. It was the home my mother had traveled over three thousand miles to perform a blessing for.

Reality was: I had to accept the offer to sell the house, find a place to live, and move forward. It was during this time that I was driving all over to find an apartment to move to, hoping the sale of the home would be enough to cover the rent. The time was running out and I had asked my relatives if I could move in with them until I could stand on my feet. Answers came back that I didn't expect. There was no room to move in and that I could live in a shelter for women.

In disbelief, I was hurt but I wasn't going to give up. I decided to take my final ride to a familiar location. I pulled my car into a parking spot at the leasing office of the apartment complex I'd lived in years before when I first moved to California.

There was my angel named Jay, the maintenance man for the complex. He called my name and I turned around as I was walking towards the office. I hugged him. Overcome with emotion, I started crying and told him my predicament. I didn't notice that he was walking with me into the leasing office. Before I could open my mouth, Jay started talking and introduced me to the leasing manager. He told her I was a personal friend that used to live there and he would vouch for me.

I filled out an application, gave copies of my bank statements and the seller's agreement from the sale of my house. I left that office with an apartment, no deposit required, and a date to move in.

I still had no job, no money in my bank accounts, and the house hadn't closed yet. My realtor offered to loan me the money to move and pay her back from the sale of the home.

I was preparing for the move, packing boxes, and selling furniture when the phone rang in my home office. When I answered, it was a recruiter. He explained he found my resume on the internet, and wanted to know if I was interested in a position he had.

I had been self-employed, working full time during the final year my mother was alive. When she was declining, my focus was on her. After she died, I had no motivation to go into my office and work. If I didn't work, no funds were coming into the home. The position he described was exactly what I was doing. No overhead and I could transfer my clientele. There was one hitch. I would have to start at entry level and my salary would reflect that of someone starting out, and not based on years of experience. I figured what did I have to lose, it was better than zero.

I moved into the apartment across from the field where I could see horses. It didn't have much sunlight, and it reflected my mood. DARK!

I started the new job at the call center, meeting new people who wanted to help me. And, there were opportunities for advancement. While in orientation I met a manager, Edward Harris, who was very spiritual. He invited himself to sit with the group at lunch. It was during lunch that he kept asking questions about my background and wanted to know if I wanted to be a manager. I was adamant that was the furthest thing from my mind because I had been burned being a manager before. I remember his words: "If it's in you, that's who you are."

It was within six months of working for the company when there were changes within the organization relating to the call center. The call center was closing: employees were being offered severance packages, offered other call center positions hours away, and there was a lift-off of the eighteen months criteria for call center employees who wanted to apply for any position.

One morning my supervisor told me to check my email, she had sent me something. I logged into my computer and there was a job requisition for a supervisor position in a district office. I applied and within days I got the job and was promoted. I thought about what Edward had said, "If it's in you, that's who you are." I am a leader.

I had received notification the new owner of my home had received my old mail. And, if I wouldn't mind to stop by and pick it up. It felt strange now, being the guest in what was once my home.

I pulled into the guest parking, walked up to my door, rung the doorbell and waited. It was answered by a friendly, older single African American woman who had purchased the home. She offered me a glass of water and a seat on the couch as she walked away. I am sitting there in the living room, my eyes looking around the room and I see a picture that I recognize.

When she returns, I accept the glass of water. "You know my pastor's daughter?"

She laughs. "That is my granddaughter."

Since I was a new member to the church, I didn't know she was my pastor's stepdaughter. She proceeded to explain the relationship, and I exhaled. She noticed and I told how I had posted a flier of the house listing at church.

I had prayed that the house was sold before it was foreclosed. God answers prayers.

So it seems that my life is slowly coming back. I have a job that is rewarding, have an apartment, and I am alive. The attorney found a way that a settlement that I was expecting wasn't impacted and it arrived in 2008. I am writing my bucket list of what I want to accomplish and it starts with writing a book.

I decided I wanted to challenge myself and write about my experiences. I had been writing in my journal about losing my mother, my house, and the ordeal of starting all over. I even started writing about how I had given up on life, wanting to die. It was through this writing experience that so much that I had tucked away from my past was coming forth. I kept the journal hidden; it wasn't time to let the world know. But the pages were filling.

During this time I enrolled in the African American Leadership program at work. It was an experience where I was able to meet others within the company to share our experiences of working in corporate America. As an African American female, I was able to share how I was perceived as the angry black woman. I was viewed as having a chip on my shoulder. When I voiced my opinion, I was considered angry. This was far from the truth and I needed to know how to handle it. I mentioned in one of the weekly meetings how I was told that I rolled my eyes. I would attend monthly management meetings, dressed professional, taking notes, and alert. I would participate in the meeting and then return to the office where my manager had been reprimanded because they said I rolled my eyes.

So I attended meetings, kept my head down and doodled so that I wasn't accused of rolling my eyes. It's in these meetings where I listened and gave my input. No one hears what I said until the next person in the room paraphrased my comments. And, then it was acknowledged. In my anger, I vowed to invest in myself and began gathering information on obtaining a master's degree. I went to my immediate manager who discouraged my going back to school; she advised the company didn't reimburse employees for anything pertaining to their education. She added I was safe in my position.

Again while at the weekly leadership meeting, I voiced concerns over my manager's statement. I was quickly informed there *was* tuition reimbursement, that my manager was probably intimidated by the thought I would become a peer. Once I was aware of the information and guided on what to say, I enrolled in the university. The rest was history. My manager signed off, and I was going to get my masters!

I decided at a family function to share with my siblings that I had been accepted—with tuition reimbursement—if I maintained a certain G.P.A. And how happy I was about the program. My sister visiting from Maryland laughed the hardest. I looked and two others were laughing as well. It was a joke at my expense. They literally thought I was kidding because when I was going for my undergraduate degree it was a struggle. Not because I wasn't smart enough, but because I didn't apply myself. As the saying goes, what doesn't kill you makes you stronger. Since I felt no one believed in my capabilities, it was up to me to prove them wrong.

During the time I pursued my studies, the classes, the teams, and the assignments were a mirror of what I had endured in my work experiences. Going through the curriculum was like a play written about my corporate life and I was the actor acting out the scene.

For the first time in my life, I had a 3.0 G.P.A. which is considered a B. In school, I was always the average grade student and didn't apply myself, because I knew I could skate by. This was different because I had something to prove. Not to anyone else, but to myself. I could hear my father in my ear "You know so much watching TV shows, why don't you show me this with your grades."

It was during one of my midterm's late nights before the Christmas holiday in 2010 that I had gone to the doctor. I questioned why my menstrual cycle had not returned after having surgery in 2008 for fibroids. Several other doctors I'd seen had been unable to get the records from the surgery and told me to just wait. It would return.

The physician assistant had told me one nurse in particular was excellent in obtaining medical records. Since my obstetrician seemed to be withholding information about the surgery, she'd assist in getting answers. She called and set the appointment for December 30, 2010, the anniversary of my mother's passing. I didn't say anything but felt that it was a sign.

The physician assistant sat across from me and read the notes from the operation and explained that I wouldn't ever be able to have children. She reported the lining of my uterus had been burned and there were no hopes for a baby. The baby I felt I had time to have when I was established in my career. The baby that when I got married, had the white picket fence and two car garage, I would have.

I sat there in disbelief that here I was getting my masters to advance in my career, prove to everyone that I had brains and could advance. I was preparing for the future where I could now support the child I wanted. My window of opportunity had closed; it had no mercy.

I got home in a daze and cried until my eyes were bloodshot. And I was feeling regret for the decisions I'd made earlier about the child I would have had. My mother had said it was okay, even thought it was a sin to have a baby out of wedlock. She was gone now almost four years. I had gone through hell and back and nothing was lining up. I had baby names already picked out: Allen, if a boy, and Alana, for a girl.

So the doctor suggested if I really wanted to have a child to think about a surrogate mother, having an egg donor, or just be content without having the child that I wanted. The cost for the surrogate would be around thirty thousand dollars and I was considering how I could make it happen.

The child never materialized, but during the late night hours there was a secret revealed. There was a child coming forth, not from myself but from the one closest to me—the one that I always called my own.

When my niece delivered her son within two weeks of my bad news, I stopped being depressed and looked into his eyes as I held him. I was going to spoil him like he was my own and look at this as a lesson. I had to find a way to forgive myself, because the clock had stopped. If I had had the child I was supposed to years earlier, would I have been able to devote my time, mental awareness, and life to my ailing mother? The answer was "no" because I had seen how my siblings who were married and had other commitments had less time.

My mother was my baby that I spoiled, loved, and did what God had intended me to do. Honor her! Now seeing this little boy, I had a reason to want to be here more than before. I wanted to see him become a man who was loved by many.

It was also during this time that I had another health scare. I was staying up late writing a term paper to turn in for a school assignment. I took my right hand and rested it under my left arm pit and noticed a lump. I finished the paper and went to do another self-examination, and the lump was the size of a pea.

I had an appointment with my primary doctor on Monday and would mention it to her. She'd placed her hand where I said the lump was and immediately I was sent for a mammogram. Everything was going so fast that when the tests came back, she wanted a biopsy done. All I could think about was that cancer ran in my family and I didn't want to die then. Now I had something to live for. While the technician was preparing me for the biopsy, I was praying. She explained they were only going to take two or three samples. The doctor came in, there were snipping sounds, and at least ten samples taken. I agonized over the weeks, waiting for the results. I finally could not take it and left a message that I needed to know before Christmas. I received the call on Christmas Eve: it wasn't cancer and they would leave the lump.

I focused on finishing my degree, earning credentials at work, and trying to build a life that I was going to live to the fullest. I was excited to submit how I wanted my name to appear on my degree, ordering my cap and gown. I was overcoming doubt, proving to others I was capable, and I was letting the sun shine on me.

The proudest moment came in July, 2011 when four of my siblings came to my graduation. Seeing them cheering in the stands when my name was called. Going up to the podium to be knighted and receiving my degree. I, the daughter of Oscar: who had a sixth grade education. None of his children had diplomas past high school, and I was there not feeling better than them, but representing them. It was for them.

I was crying tears of joy because I came from a long line of strong African American women. I remember as a child seeing a picture of my sisters that was in the newspaper. The article was about how they all had received their degrees: associates, Bachelor of Science and one with her masters. They had earned scholarships, worked full time, and been awarded grants to fulfill their dreams of getting an education. There I was, the one who was an average student, growing up and walking across the stage with my masters. I belonged!

I felt that I had accomplished one of my dreams by getting my masters. What was next? I had gone through the storm, I had no kids to carry on my legacy, and I was wondering, *what if I've inherited the ugly disease called dementia? What if I can no longer remember? What if my words don't come one day? What would my legacy be?* I am remembering my mother, the ordained minister. She left us with so many memories, but her sermons written in notebooks were what triggered something. We were able to see her thought process as she'd scripted the words to deliver to save souls. I am not a minister, but it was at that time that I had the idea, *what about my words? What if I can write about my experiences through my poetry?* I went to my nightstand and there it was…my journal. Pieces of paper tucked between pages, words that were shared only in those pages, and secrets that I'd kept. I picked up the pen and let the words flow. I felt alive and decided I would let my words be my legacy when I was gone.

I decided in March, 2012 to release my first book of poetry, *Through the Fire,* which debuted my mission. I was writing about losing my mother, the grief I was going through, and the first birthday she wouldn't be there to wish me a Happy Birthday. I was introducing to the world my words that I had kept hidden.

I wrote about the experiences of falling in love with the wrong men in my life and the special one that I had let walk away.

There was poetry that I wrote about Oscar Grant, a young African American male, gunned down in California on New Year's Eve by a Bart police officer. And, the convicted officer sentenced to two years, that led to my questioning the system of a man getting a lesser sentence for killing a man and others receiving life sentences for a crime that deserved less time.

I wrote about the obstacles my mother overcame and why I adored her. She was my hero, not just because she was my parent, but because of what she stood for. A trailblazer before her time. At her funeral, many stood to offer accolades for her accomplishments that paved the way for others.

Lastly, I had to write about those I felt had left me, the faith I had lost. And to realize that when everyone had walked out, there was someone always there. I was looking in the wrong direction, and He was always placing people in my life to show me. My mother had laid the foundation by always taking me to church. Though I had grown older and strayed away from the church when the trials and tribulations came, I cried thousands of tears. I had forgotten that there was a higher power to bring me out.

The following year I had lost family members to cancer, others were being diagnosed with cancer, and I was doing my own self-evaluation of who I really am. I wrote another book of poetry called *Loving Me.*

This time I faced talking about being bullied as a child and how that impacted me as an adult. I was seeing in the media so many children were ending their lives at early ages because they would rather face death than another day of being bullied. I had to express the hurt I was feeling for them.

Also, I'd started to share my feelings of being in a relationship with someone that I needed to leave in order to be free for someone to find me to love and respect. I didn't have the strength yet to do that. So I would try to meet others, but my heart wasn't open to receive them, because it was still tied up to the man that was unavailable.

The poetry revealed experiences I had gone through, that someone had shared with me, or I imagined. I was looking in the mirror and seeing that I had always taken care of others and with the devastating loss of my mother, I didn't know how to take care of myself.

I had gone on vacation for seven days and when I was done had written the majority of the book. Because I had to begin with loving myself in order for those coming into my life to know at what level of love I would accept.

I had shared with the public my fear of getting Alzheimer's and how I was committing to writing a book a year until the pen stops. I started fearing forgetting, thinking that dementia was creeping up on me. I was paranoid and missing a flight, forgetting where I left a pair of earrings, or misplacing my checkbook was overcoming my being. I was becoming afraid of aging.

My next book was called *Let It Rain* and some didn't understand the meaning. I realized that it didn't matter what others thought. I accepted myself for who I was—a plus size African American Queen, strong minded, and understanding that the challenges that life threw at me were not to distract me, but make me stronger. I had to look for the good in everything that had happened. I had to learn to forgive. I had to look at the sensual side of becoming older, maturer, and comfortable in myself. There was someone that I was addicted to and I had to build up enough strength to walk away. But could I? As the door was between us and I heard his heartbeat, I couldn't resist.

Turning fifty years old meant that I was half a century old. I had wisdom and choices. I was reflecting on my life, the decisions that I had made, my purpose and where I was going. (Davis, 2005) It was at this age that I decided to plan for my party, a year in advance. I had everything planned even to the details of what was on the table. I had purchased eleven dresses until the right one was in my possession. I felt that I was marrying myself. I was making a commitment to myself that regardless if I ever met someone who loved me, I loved me better.

I had mentioned to the man who I slept with every Tuesday about my party, but I didn't invite him because I didn't want to be disappointed again. I didn't want to see him come—to leave early. I didn't want to keep watching the door for his arrival—for him to not arrive. And, I didn't want him—to be the center of my attention. I wanted to be loved! I wanted to celebrate live! I wanted it to rain!

I remember going to Atlanta to a book conference and selling my books. This book has sold the most, because I stated that when prayers go up, blessings come down. I wanted it to rain! I felt energized, and so when my mentee invited me to a popular spot called the Apache Café, where other authors, spoken word artists performed, I was excited, yet intimidated. My niece, mentee, and friends arrived and I was a little nervous, because I didn't know if I would be accepted. I decided to do a spoken word piece called "My Inner Freak."

Nothing anyone expected from this fifty-year-old professional woman from California. Stepping onto the stage, I was no longer myself, but my alter ego Blessed Poet Pat! I began speaking the words, slowing down at times, so they could take the ride with me, and climaxing at the very moment I had them.

It was at this moment I knew I didn't have the disease. I was aging like the rest of the universe. I was to enjoy the time that I had and smell all the roses. The fear of dying, getting older, and anything else had to leave.

I was writing books and going through struggles at the same time. I was writing in my old journal, crying many tears, and found three cards in my jewelry box. They were inscribed with the words *This Too Shall Pass* and I dedicated the next book to my two sisters and my best friend who wrote the note cards to me.

Those cards came when I was considering suicide. I was losing the house my mother had prayed over, so I felt I'd lost it all, and I felt that my siblings—who all had the same parents except myself—had left me. Those cards were telling me I would make it. I just didn't see it at the time I was in the storm.

The book covered making it through the storm, and I was hoping the readers who had followed me from the very beginning saw there was light at the end of the tunnel.

Hopefully, those men and women were rooting for me to leave the man who was my crack alone. They had gone through it and came through, but wanted *me* to finally let it go! Once I felt that I was drowning, and he needed more than I could give—I had to let him go! I had to save myself. When I did, it seemed that everything else fell into place. I bought the mattress on a limb, and the salesperson was determined to help—even missed her ride home. She wanted to make sure that I never again had to sleep on the mattress he and I had shared. That old mattress wouldn't stay in my house another month. When the delivery men came into my home to deliver the new mattress, I was like a kid waiting for a new beginning.

I was glad to see the mattress that he and I shared go. I was glad to see it ride off on the back of that truck.

There was so much I learned about myself writing that book. I learned about life, love and death. I found that those reading the book related to it for so many reasons. They would email me, message me, and do reviews about how they could relate to the poetry and letters and more that I shared. I wrote about a "Call from Heaven," where I wished I could speak one more time to my mother. I talked to her about everything—not that I couldn't with my father. But with a mother, there is a different relationship.

I wish God could just let the call come through for me to hear her voice, ask her questions, and tell her about what I was going through so she could comment. Readers related to that, because we all have mothers and we can only imagine.

The other piece that I wrote about, being that I am a preacher's kid, was the "Calling," where you felt that you must be obligated to carry on the tradition. I felt that I must be called to be a preacher. I have my mother's clergy robe, I go to church, and I read the bible. The struggle that I have is: *could I be responsible for lost souls?* And I don't know if I can answer the call. I remember the struggle my mother, being a female, faced and the tears she shed.

I can still picture her coming home after driving to New Jersey with my brother and father. She was in the living room and they were consoling her. I snuck into the background to listen. She was crying and saying, "How could they embarrass me like that"? She had come that far to receive her license to preach, and they only had her come to tell her "No." Even in the male-dominated clergy world, a woman couldn't have received the *Call,* and if she did they were going to make sure she was restricted. I would have dreams, I would not answer the *Call,* and I would keep the robe in the back of the closet safe.

I took a year off from writing a book because I felt that I was contemplating. Was this vision of mine done in vain, or was there a purpose bigger than myself? I was self-doubting my ability, and it held me hostage.

It was during this time that my life took a turn. It seemed like the time when I was the happiest is when the trouble crept back in. I was traveling from Utah, Hawaii, Atlanta, and Connecticut. I was determined to see the world, expose everyone to my books, as well as take care of myself.

PART 5

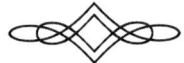

You Will One Day Understand

Until you bury your parents, you will never understand
The grief will rock you to the core
When I see a mother and daughter out and about, I always smile. Wishing that
my mother was still alive and we had our special moments to laugh, hug, and get
my kiss on the cheek. I sometimes will stop the daughter and tell her to treat her
mother good, because I miss my mother. They will nod their heads, getting the
message, because they see the hurt in my eyes.

Or to see a father and daughter makes me remember being the apple of my
father's eye. There's a special bond of being a daddy's girl, the feeling of being
protected, talking about my goals and aspirations to be great and him encouraging
me. When I see others taking their parents for granted, I find myself getting angry
and waiting to tell them I'd rather trade places and have my parents still alive and
well, than to be my guardian angels.

One Wish

I have one wish before I die

I want to wake up with no aches and pains

I want to feel the warmth of the sun against my skin

I want to hear him breathing softly beside me

I want to wander down to the kitchen where I read the newspaper, and there is no war anywhere

I have a wish that we aren't divided

I have a wish that the love between us all is enough to keep us alive

I don't want to die

I have a wish to travel the world, taking photos of the moment

Like a child seeing something for the first time. Being inquisitive

I want to wake up from the nightmare where a child doesn't make it home

There isn't a bomb being dropped over a school, killing innocent children to make a point. The question is to whom? A leader? A race?

I have a wish that we are all free

Running along the beach

Wind blowing in our hair

Happy

In Love

Feeling that if it ends tomorrow

At least we know that it wasn't in vain, that we were free to be and we had one wish

To feel peace

I Rise Up

Like dust on the floor
You left me
Not realizing the power that was within me
I gather myself
Go back to my sanctuary and I pray
I had forgotten who I was
I am the nurturer
I am the backbone
I am the one who puts everything together
So I had to reassess the situation
When you threw words at me to hurt me
When my self-esteem was put into a chamber
I had to say, "NO"!
Enough is enough
I took my black suit out of the closet
That's right—Tahari
It still fits
Slide my pedicured toes into my four-inch black Jimmy Choo shoes
Dressed for success
Meeting at 1 p.m.
What you thought was for bad
A power greater than you made it right for me
I Rise Up
And sit upon my throne

The Message

I run into the home and pick up the receiver
I remember the phone number by heart
I dial each number
The phone rings and the answering machine clicked on. I leave a message
I say, "Hi Mommy, I miss you
I love you so much. Call me back!"
I hang up and pass out
A couple of hours pass by
I am awakened by the phone ringing
It is your number
My heartbeat speeds up
I answer, "Mommy"!
There is a voice I don't recognize on the other end
They say, "I am sorry, but you must have the wrong number
The reason why I am calling is because you keep calling this number and leaving
messages.
I hope you find your mother
I hope she calls you back."
The tears form in my eyes
I can barely see
I say, "Thank you for calling back," and "I am sorry for the inconvenience."
My mother is gone
She passed away
I was hoping it was a dream
I was hoping that she would call me back
I hang up
The tears flow

The Wedding

Since I was a little girl
I imagined this day
I have practiced with my dolls
Walking down the aisle
White gown, long train, and the bouquet of flowers that smelled like heaven
When I got older, I had a notebook
In it were all the details of the wedding
I would have it at this church
It was going to be a big wedding
I was going to have Daddy walk me down the aisle
He passed away, so I made the adjustments
I would have *all* my brothers walk me down the aisle
This was adjusted, too, as the years spanned
And each brother had passed away, too, only one left
I had so many girlfriends, the colors were set
Even told them the way I wanted their pedicures to look
As soon as I had a new love in my life, the call would be made to each. We would giggle and I said I will let you know.
We were all excited, thinking the day would come
As I got older, the friends became fewer, decisions on choosing the right one for me were more important.
I kept making adjustments to the notebook until I finally threw it in the trash
I figured that it would be a small wedding
If he loves me, it can be at my sibling's home. Mother could perform the ceremony, and they could be the witnesses.
It stopped being about the wedding, and it became about who really loves me
Would I be settling just to be married?
Would I be happy?
Would I marry someone who cheated on me?
All these things ran through my mind.
Finally my mother passed
Never seeing me walk down the aisle
Married couples discouraging me to stay single and never married
I look at them and shake my head

As they prepare to go to bed each night in each other's arms, and I lie holding my pillow tight

Love Over Everything

So often we feel alone
Forgetting that there is always the first love
FAMILY
When friends walk out
When there are trials
When you question who to trust
There is always family
No matter if large or small
Choose love over everything
I had to be reminded
I thought that this thing we call life
I had to go it alone
Go through the good, the bad, the ugly
Holding in all the emotion
Not sharing anything with anyone
Almost about to blow
Feeling broken
It is during this time that I am reminded
That family always is there
Never asking for a thank you
Family doesn't need a thank you
Because it's love over everything
If I love you, then it's sincere
If I love you, I am not looking for anything in return
If I am looking for a handout, then I am not family
I sit in my chair and my head nods
I remember
I was taught better
And I am proud of my family
I am leading by example
Never realizing that my mistakes are their maps
It's Love over Everything

I Made A Mistake

I made the mistake of thinking that you care
I forgot that it is every man for himself
As I laid on the operation table
Taking in the gas to put me under
I am thinking, *where is he?*
He was supposed to be the last one I looked at
I was supposed to tell you I loved you
I was supposed to hear you say, "I love you, babe"
Instead, I have my sister driving me to the hospital
Telling me it will be okay
And someone will be here when you awake to take you home
I spent years with this man
I thought I knew him
I thought that he would fight for me
Not give up on us and go back to her
I made a mistake and I can't get it back
I loved him and he let me go
Finally after all these years, he heard what I asked for
But I made a mistake!!!

Something for Boom Boom Room

Baby, I didn't forget about you

I showered in Bath & Body Works Sensual Amber body wash from head to toe.

Glistening from the water before drying off

Looking in the mirror

Admiring the tone muscles from our daily workouts

The fullness of my breasts

Everything is smooth for you, baby

Don't have to worry about any follicles in your warm mouth

French manicure and toes painted OPI Black Onyx

Candles lit all over the Boom Boom Room

Lights off and all you smell is me

Pandora is softly playing the station "Legs Shakin Radio"

Pertois Moriset Cuvee Selection Sparkling Wine is chilling in the ice bucket

You are my best friend

You are my lover

Every day is a new beginning

I never thought I could be this happy

This much in love

This turned on by hearing your voice

Telling me as you are driving home everything that you are going to do to me

I hear the key turn in the door

As I hear you walk up the stairs, my heartbeat quickens

Quick spray of lavender oil onto the sheets

Slide my feet into four-inch black patent leather Christian Louboutin "So Kate" pumps

The door opens to the Boom Boom Room and your eyes light up

I surprised you again

Nothing on but the pumps

I motion for you to come over and take a seat

I proceed to give you a lap dance

Sneaking a kiss between a thrust of my hips

Another kiss on your forehead while I let my breasts dangle in front of your mouth for a flick of your tongue

I turn around and face the mirror seeing our reflections looking back at me

In the Boom Boom Room, we promised each other

That we would please each other until we fall asleep

We said that it's a marathon

I love seeing you getting excited

As you slip out of your jacket, you whisper sweet nothings in my ear

As your tie and shirt come off, I feel your hands moving faster

I step towards the mirror and dance for you

I turn back to you and I say, "Do you like what you see?"

Head nods up and down

You motion for me to come to you

As I walk toward you with my heels still on

I lick my lips and as I stroll to you, I see you are pouring a glass of sparkling wine

Your hand comes up to my mouth with the glass. I take a sip

You then ask me to lie on the bed

Keep the heels on

You pour some of the sparkling wine between my breasts and lick it up

Pour some more so that it rests in my belly button and sip

You pour the remaining sparkling wine between my legs and proceed to lick every drop of wine from my sweet spot

As I moan and cry out with pleasure

You smile at me

"You like being in the Boom Boom Room?"

With a raspy voice, I said, "I love this as long as it's with you"

As you undress and climb upon the bed, my legs open wider

Heels pointed to the ceiling

Music seems to get louder

Or maybe it was me getting lost in emotion

As we ride the tidal wave of lust

The movement intensifies

There! Right there. That spot right there

We both climax

Collapse on top of the sheets

Smelling the faint smell of lavender

You look down at my feet and notice the heels never came off and you smile

You take one shoe off and pour some sparkling wine between my toes and as you taste each toe I scream for you stop

We giggle and know that we have met each other's match

Blessed to be your wife and love that you're my husband
And that we get to visit the Boom Boom Room

Keep Living

As I listen to my elders, I am complaining about everything
They say, "Keep living"
You're complaining about aches and pains
They, being much older, not complaining, but being thankful
You, waking up and complaining about your job and the treatment
The elders again shaking their heads and saying, "Baby, keep living"
Calling them on the phone and complaining about the treatment in your
relationships
Pause on the other end of the phone, and then they say, "Keep living"
Finally face to face, you ask, "Why, whenever you have anything that is causing
you pain, hurt, or mistreatment, do you keep saying, 'Keep living'?"
The elder smiles and explains:
"There is someone who didn't wake up this morning
You're complaining about aches and pains, but you're still here
You complain about a job that you applied to work at daily
Yet the treatment you are going through is never like those who came before you.
The shoulders you're standing on are those who had to work more than eight-
hour shifts, no breaks and lunches. There wasn't a labor board monitoring their
treatment. They went to work and took the treatment because they had families to
support.
The reason I said to keep living is because the world isn't done with you yet. There
is a lesson in everything you have to experience. Stop and look at what is handed
to you.
It won't always be difficult
There will be good times
Keep living!"

Put Respect on My Name

I am not your side chick
I am not the other woman
I am the one when the world tore you down
When they told you, you were not worth anything; I stood there with arms open
telling you that you mean the world to me.
So when we were out and we came across your friends
Why couldn't I be introduced to them?
Why was I your friend?
When you needed me, I was there
When you had nothing, I poured into you
I opened my heart
Remember my name
Respect me as the woman I am
Put respect on my name

Sometimes It Hurts

When you have done all you can
You can't blame anyone
You just have to realize, it's the best for each
Ending a relationship for the best
So that you both are at peace
After the tears have dried
The anger has subsided
You pick up the pieces
You put on a mask
Pretend to your friends that you're okay
When you're alone
Sipping on your glass of chardonnay
Looking out the window
You can be yourself
You can admit to yourself
That even though it was the best
It hurts
There are times that you just want to be held
You just want to be loved
You just want to hear the key in the door
See him walk in
That's not going to happen anymore
Sometimes it hurts so badly
That you just want to change your name
Move to another location
Don't want to risk seeing him
Sometimes it hurts
Feels like shards of glass
Scraping against my skin
The pain doesn't dull

Being Alone

I sit here looking at the seat next to me
Tired of waiting for someone to be there
I am good being alone
Really?
I travel the world
I purchased everything that should have been done for us
House
Car
Bad Boss Lady
Intimidating to others
Can't wait
Can't wait to bring out the china
Can't wait to bring out the furs and diamonds
Being okay with the queen that I am
It would be nice to share this estate with a king
But I am getting older and I got to live
I got to love myself
I can't settle for the name of MRS.
I can be a MISS and be at peace
Didn't turn out how I expected
The chapter isn't over yet
Until he comes
I am okay with being happy with myself alone!

It's Here

Now I am at the age where I am enjoying life

Daily I see where people my age are dying

It made me realize that reality is here

I am not as young as I think

My body is letting me know

My mind thinks it's younger

Another peer quickly fighting for another breath

I am thankful for each morning

They are deciding on their funeral arrangements

I am thinking about my next vacation

They are starting Go Fund Me accounts

I am shaking my head

Not Me!

Speaking to elders, they explain this is the reality

You're at the age now where more peers will be dying than celebrating another
birthday

I am waking up

I finally let it hit me like a brick wall when it's someone close to me dies

I need to take better care of myself

I need to have everything in order

I need to be thankful for each

Sunrise

I need to stop for each sunset

I need to let those who are important to me know it

It's here

Saving The Cookies

I can remember like it was yesterday
I said I was done
I wasn't going to wait on you to decide
What would it mean?
No more Tuesday escapades
No more waiting
I would be first for the right one
My sweet spot would not be wet for you
I would have to save it
Don't think about you
Not your girth
Not your morning wake up calls
Not hearing that deep baritone voice
Was it worth it?
I miss you from afar
I still look at your text messages
I still look at the videos
I still look at the pictures
Just talking about you makes my heart skip a beat
I could settle, but it's not worth it
I make light of it
I stay focused on goals
Things that I didn't think about with you
Instead of being bitter
I am sweet
I save each cookie
Until the right one comes to taste

Cabo

On the flight
Treated like a queen
Landed and the greeting is bliss
I feel like Oprah
I arrive at the location
Doors opened
Champagne flowing
The ocean is welcoming
The experience is life changing
I bathe with the windows open
I awake daily with the sunrise on my pillow
I hear you
I wish you were with me in more ways than one
Visiting the hot spots
Locals smiling
I made up my mind and I am free

Ten Years

I am thinking about the ten years and what I have learned.

I am free. I feel like it's a mid-life crisis

I don't want to get your approval

I don't need your approval

I am sitting here ten years later

I am thinking that I don't need to impress anyone

I am too old to play games

You can't make me feel like the slave that you thought I was

I know who I am

I am at the age where people are dying off

Cancer is the new norm

I'd rather have a drink

A tall glass of whiskey

Don't nobody got time for dying

It's been ten years since you have left

I know better

I know that I won't accept the scraps from the table

I know that I deserve more

So when life throws the lemons at me

The lemonade is made with a shot of patron

It's been ten years since you have left

I have gone to hell and back

I have had to fight for what is mine

I have been lied on

I have been tested

I realized who has my back

Who have been users who have shown up

It's been ten years

Though you are in a better place

I have had to realize that they would come for me

That I would have to be wiser

I can't get comfortable

I have to stay on my game

Don't want to lose my mind

Don't want to forget this time
It's been ten years and I got the scars to show

Scab

It's been over ten years
I have all the documents about you put neatly away
To the point that I don't have to memorize anything
I just know that you passed, I grieved, and I am okay
It wasn't until a relative needed to know the exact
Reason for your passing that I had to face my biggest fear
I had to look through those documents
Your medical records
Your final years
I looked in one spot where I knew everything would be at
It wasn't there and feared that I had lost my memory
Had I misplaced it beyond finding?
I needed to find this to help another, so the pressure is on
Like a teakettle slowing simmering
I am sweating, I can't sleep, and I feel my heartbeat about to jump out of my chest
It's the day before it is needed
Like a scab I rip off the bandage
There is a box hidden away
I remember the backup
I open the box
I fumble through the pages
Some fall at my feet
The tears streaming down my face
First page enrollment
Last page discharged
The blood is rushing to my head
I feel like I can't breathe
I feel like I am going to faint
The scab that was to cover up the feelings
Has been pulled off completely
A flood of emotions covers me
I remember why I tucked away the box
I didn't want to feel the pain
I had increased my habit because I wanted to check out
I had wanted to die, too

She couldn't breathe
Her lungs didn't want to work any longer
I wanted to exhale and take the last breath
Why did I pull off the scab?

Plus 1

You're single
You're invited to events
You don't want to go solo
On a rampage to find a Plus 1
Asking friends, relatives, and even coworkers
Don't want to be asked are you still single?
Don't want to be asked are you straight?
Is there something wrong with you?
So you're feeling bad about being you
You're feeling bad about being a successful you
You're feeling at this point no one loves you
You're getting caught up in their drama
You're asking God what happened to your Plus 1.
Something happens and it's like a light has been turned on.
You realize that no matter where you go and who you are with, you're loved.
You boldly reply to invitations and attend solo and if there is a Plus 1, there is no pressure
You just got someone else to do the cupid shuffle with

Happy Anniversary

It's been ten years since we laid you to rest
Dust to dust were the final words I remembered
Can't go to your final resting place
Got the lot number, marker number, and still I got lost trying to find the cemetery
Instead of taking a left, I went right
Thought I knew the location and it was a different cemetery all together
I thought I was finally accepting that you're gone
The tears well up in my eyes. I can't do it!
Making all your dishes so that the house smells like you
Running to my siblings for acceptance
Does it taste like hers?
Seeing them inspect, take a forkful, close their eyes, and the smiles spread across their faces
Feeling the love for the moment
Remembering all the special meals you made for us over the years
Thinking about all the challenges you overcame is my benchmark
If you could sacrifice for your family to accomplish your goals, I know I can do it
I know whatever I am going through, I can make it because I remember you
I keep thinking about the stories you shared
The strong woman who you were, to endure so that I can be here
I am your offspring
I ran to the store
Went to the bakery
Found the perfect cake
Your favorite
Got a candle, lit the match, and the flame lit the cake
Happy Anniversary, Mommy

It's Almost a Year

Don't think about him or the feelings will overcome you
You shake it off
You hear in the faint distance his voice
Only to realize it's your imagination
Your body aches in the middle of the night for his touch
His hands to caress your body
Feel the heat from his body next to yours
It's so hot you turn on the fan because you realize he's gone.
Never coming back unless you pick up the phone
You need to close that chapter
You need to open your heart
You need to move on
At times you want to dial his number that you have etched in your memory
Drive by his house, but you can't
You already know the answer
You awake daily and the desires return

Another Angel Got Their Wings

Daily I post my condolences to you and your family

Sometimes it's two to three families that have lost a loved one

I feel their pain, no matter their age, no matter the gender

You grieve for them

From the gunshot to natural causes, someone has left their earthly body

You question God. "Why?"

Been there and trust me, you don't want to know the answer.

You need to make funeral arrangements

You don't want to let them go

You don't want to say goodbye, but see you soon

You put your white outfit on for the homegoing

Walk with your head held high and you pray

Pray for strength to make it through

Celebrate their lives

You smile and say another angel has gotten their wings

The gate opened

We're left here waiting our turn

Let Me Drink Your Bath Water

There is enough love to make you drunk
My baby leaves me notes on my pillow
Rose petals all over the floor
Scented candles light up the whole house
Chilled strawberries next to the king-size bed
Warm water fills the claw foot tub
He extends his hand
Don't lose your balance
Take one step in
French-pedicured toes immersed into water feels so good
As I sit down
His eyes brighten
He says I love every part of you
Everything about you is beautiful
He sees no flaw
As the ladle comes out of the bowl next to the tub
He says you're so sweet
Dips it into the bathwater
As I giggle
He takes a sip

Knocking At The Door

Living my life
Not focusing on the man sitting on the sidewalk
Walk past him
Not hearing him plead for spare change
Rolling up my window as I approached the red light
Don't make eye contact with the homeless family
Coming up to the window asking for change
Thinking that I am better
Don't want to help my fellow brother or sister
Never thinking that it could be me
I automatically think I go to church every Sunday
I don't volunteer to help with any auxiliaries
I don't even want to hold other's hands
Time is up
I transition
I am at the Pearlie gates
It's beautiful
Just like I imagined
Golden streets
Big mansions
Others are knocking
The door is swung open
Greeted by their loved ones
I step up to the gate and knock
Excited for the door to be opened and I see my loved ones
I knock harder
I feel ashamed as I realized what is transpiring
The door isn't opened for me
My life flashed before me as I am judged
The faces of each I ignored
A tear runs down my face
Knuckles bloodied
Lord, forgive me!

Stop Waiting

Waiting for the special day
Don't eat off that china
Save it
Don't wear those diamonds
Let them sparkle when you go some place
Save your money for that rainy day
Keep cutting out pictures of places you want to go
Bucket list getting longer
Don't sit in the living room, that's for special guests
That new restaurant that everyone is going to
You dream of going one day
Your favorite dish is lasagna
You only eat it for special occasions
Those red bottoms or whatever shoes you saw in the magazine
You've seen them in the store, looked at the price tag, put them back
As you age and the reality settles in
The gray hairs appear around your temple
You got a collection building up in the garage of items for those special days
The dust is collecting on your dreams
Finally you come home
Open the windows
Let the fresh air in
New hairdo
Vacation planned
China set daily
Diamonds sparkle in each earlobe
You're living in the now
Stop waiting and live

Bargaining

It's a hot July summer day
It's not even time for dinner
Sitting in the hospital room
Watching like a hawk making sure everything is in place
Exhausted, but I got to be on guard
Nothing can happen while she is in my care
Visitors come and she is quiet
They pray over her and she smiles
Holding the newspaper in her hands
Notice that the pages are shaking
My head turns and out of the corner of my vision
I see she is not responsive
Fear swallows me up
Not on my watch
I grab the call button
The nurse answers
"Help," I scream
As they run into the room
I am pulled away
I start bargaining
If you let her live
I will go to church every Sunday
I will give up this and that
I will turn over a new leaf
Please don't let her go, not now!
Not on my watch!
I can't tell them she's gone
Lord, please hear me!
I hear over the intercom
Code Blue
White coats flying in the wind
Looking like wings
Doctors and nurses coming from everywhere
Deal…
She is going to be okay

They Don't Know

As a little girl, I had a crush on you
Standing in the background, I was invisible to you
You would smile when you saw me, but you didn't see me
You were the school jock, the pretty boy, the trophy for all the girls much older
than me
I would see you when you came back for visits
Always a new love on your arm
Sharing pleasantries
I realized that it would not happen in this lifetime
Years later I see you
I have filled out in places that have caught your attention
I give you a hug and introduce you to my friends
Not thinking that you are interested in me
I was insecure
Didn't know the veil had been removed
I am shining
You see me
Annual visits to be in your arms
It's a secret that we don't share with anyone
Phone calls with all the promises
Text messages with all the love emojis
You say you need me to survive
I land at the airport and you're there to greet me
Kisses that suck the life from me
As you drive one hand on the wheel
Your free hand in my honey spot
Driving to our destination
They don't know
As you park, I catch my breath
Anticipation is getting the best of me
Rushing inside
Moments stolen away
I cry in your arms, you whisper you love me, wish I was closer.
Lovemaking
Knowing every part of each other's bodies

Sleeping in total bliss

Shower

Dress

Leave

Public sees us as two

They don't know

Redbone

That's the label

Light skinned, caramel complexion, red undertone complexion

You aren't dark skinned, so you don't hear "The darker the berry, the sweeter the juice"

You aren't mulatto to pass

She's high yella, you hear them describe your friend

You hear them describing you

She's a fine-looking redbone

Got to have her

Look at her smile, with that gap between her teeth

Wide hips, Thick curls surround my face and figure like a coke bottle

Blushing

You say to him, "Are you from the South?"

A smile spreads across his face

You love those southern men

Loving Me

Walking around the house with just my heels on
Open the patio door
Step out onto the patio
Lie on the lounge chair
Sunning to toast my skin a golden brown
Not ashamed of my body
Made in His image
I am comfortable in my skin
Love every inch of myself
Loving Me
Plus size means more to love
Petite means love the small package that you are in
Just like diamonds come small
Loving every stretch mark
Eyes that will hypnotize those who look into them
Lips full with sun-kissed lip balm
There is nothing you can say to hurt me
I am beautiful like those who came before me
Nefertiti, Cleopatra, Lena
I am loving me
My hair can be natural, straight, or curly
It adorns my crown
No longer being plagued by what society accepts as beautiful

Prisoner in My Mind

As I look out the window
Trying to put the words together
I can see them, but they can't form to come out of my mouth
I know you're someone who cares for me
If only I could remember who you are
My mind is slowly forgetting things
What day is it?
Where am I?
Can you bring me home?
Sorry, I don't know the address.
Tomorrow I am back to normal
For a moment, I am able to laugh with you
Share memories of my past
Then a cloud comes over me again
Brings me back into my prison cell
Embarrassed to depend on you to clean me
Not being able to control myself
What is my world coming to?
You visit me daily
Stroking the hair away from my face
Smiling at me
Looking into my eyes
Waiting for that familiar recognition
A moan is all I can get out
You smile
I can see the words jumbled in my brain
I just can't remember how to form them
I am praying for freedom
Ready to break out of this prison
I hate this disease
Alzheimer's

Texting

Whatever I didn't have the nerve to say
I would take a shot of Don Julio tequila
I would grab my iPhone
Let the words flow from my fingertips
Texting you
The liquid courage
Everything that I held in
The words flowed
I laid it all out there on the screen
I can only imagine you reading the text messages
Funny I won't remember when I wake up

Dress Rehearsal

Years of dishonesty
Late nights of being out with the boys
Lipstick on the pillowcase
All the arguments
The makeup sex
The promises that it will be better
I hang in there
Waiting my turn
No commitment
No ring
We end it
Start again
Finally got off the Ferris wheel
Not long after reading the newspaper
You're getting married
All the tears I shed over you
Sitting telling you what you needed to improve on
That you needed to be a better communicator
You needed to be committed
You didn't apply it with the teacher
You used our relationship as a dress rehearsal…
You changed, you proposed, she accepted
I stand at the back of the church
Alone

There Is Sunshine After The Rain

What doesn't kill you makes you stronger
There had to be the storms to make you learn who to lean on
Thunderstorms at times
Flooding of tears
Friends and family testing your strength
Your mental bandwidth stretched to the point you want to snap and disconnect
No longer depending on anyone for anything
Saying you want to be loved, but afraid to be hurt, so the wall is kept up
Begging the lover to let you go, but realizing that he didn't have the strings to keep you
It was you that was afraid to walk out the door
Analyzing the who, what, and the why of every situation
Coming back from the ashes that were to kill you
Walking by faith and not by sight
The tightrope was frightening until you found yourself on the other side
Rose-tinted glasses were a fad
Putting on your new Cynthia Bailey frames, you see others for who they really are
Now not afraid of confronting them and telling them what you see
You grieve your parents at various parts of your life
Losing your mother was unexpected and felt like a scab was ripped off
You learn that it will heal in time
Your confidence intimidates others
To the point that a marker is placed on your back
You duck and dive from getting hit
Until you throw up your hands and quit
The freedom is exhilarating
You used to love the rain
The smell of the rain was like electricity going through your veins
As you walk further, the rain is getting lighter to the point it feels like a sprinkle
The umbrella is let down
You stand on the top of the hill
The sun is starting to peak through the clouds
All the:
Pain
Suffering

Disappointment

Betrayal

Loss

Gossip

Non-committed relationships

They evaporate just like they poured

It's a new day, lessons learned, and blessings came down

CONCLUSION

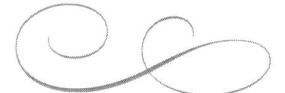

Time has flown by in the ten years since she passed. The fear of having the disease has subsided. The lessons of life have taught me to live to the fullest and take the bumps along the way as war wounds. If I forget something, there is not a panic that I have Alzheimer's, but it means that I am doing too much and need to slow down.

The job that I felt saved my life gave me accolades, but was silently killing me from the inside out. Embedded since I was a child that you don't quit, but you figure out how to win. If it meant recreate myself into someone I don't recognize, then I would put the mask on. Lesson learned that it's not always about winning, but knowing when to walk away with all the lessons and prepare for the next level.

Relationships were the hardest pill to swallow. Reflecting on how I was allowing people to make withdrawals from my life, but never making deposits. Questioning why it was acceptable to make decisions to be with someone who wasn't available. The mirror in front of me showed that I didn't want to be accountable, but wanted convenience. The feeling of acceptance was more important than being hurt by the lies, the betrayal, or worse realizing that love wasn't involved.

Many can relate to losing a loved one and how they deal with the grief varies. It's been ten years for myself. Daily, I struggled and made the decision to live versus die. Everyone knows that it is a part of life to be born into the world, be shaped by situations, make decisions on how to react, and know that eventually we will become one with dust again. When it happens to someone close to you, it feels like a piece of your heart has been ripped out and you're lowered into the ground when they are buried.

Going through life was like it was a dream, and I would wake up to the new normal. Time was speeding by, and the only document I had to show that I had witnessed it, was my words. I let them all out for the world to see. I am never professing to be perfect, but that I am still a work in progress.

Here sitting on the balcony looking out at the horizon, I am wishing that the clock would slow down. Feeling the sea breeze graze my cheek, I know that through all my trials and triumphs, it was nobody but God that brought me through when I wanted to just give up on everything.

That's when the encouragement to continue happened. There is sunshine after the rain!

RESOURCES

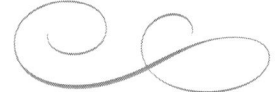

Signs Of Dementia

1. Memory loss. This is usually the earliest and most noticeable symptom.

2. Trouble recalling recent events or recognizing people and places.

3. Trouble finding the right words.

4. Problems planning and carrying out tasks, such as balancing a checkbook, following a recipe, or writing a letter.

5. Trouble exercising judgment, such as knowing what to do in an emergency.

6. Trouble controlling moods or behaviors. Depression is common, and agitation or aggression may occur. (Dementia - Symptoms, 1995)

7. Not keeping up personal care such as grooming or bathing.

Steps Of Grieving

1. **Denial** - Being in shock and feeling numb, I was able to make funeral arrangements. This stage is to protect the individual from dealing with the intensity of the loss.

2. **Bargaining** - I wanted to review all the medical records. Should I have taken her to this hospital over the other hospital where her primary had access? Was there something that I missed?

3. **Depression** - The funeral is over. I have to deal with the reality that she is gone. I wake up and go into my home office, not eating anything or drinking water until after 7 p.m. I had no appetite. I was showing up at my mother's group home, her convalescent home to see her roommate, the recreation center. I used to love to read novels and now I can't concentrate to read a paragraph. I want to stay in bed and sleep forever.

4. **Anger** - My anger was towards the people who I felt could have helped. I was angry at my siblings. I felt alone because no one understood how I felt. I went as far as fighting one sister. I couldn't be mad at my mother for leaving.

5. **Acceptance** - Through writing in my journals that later became my books, I was able to go through the steps of accepting that she was gone. She was in a better place where she didn't have to suffer. She never wanted to have feeding tubes, she had made peace with loved ones, and she was ready. After going through the healing, it was a testament that with her faith she knew she was going to heaven. Without a doubt. It made me hunger to become a better Christian. (Coping With Grief, 2005)

Signs that you are dating a married man

1. He doesn't talk about his friends.

2. He has two cell phones.

3. He calls you from odd locations.

4. He's unavailable to talk or text.

5. He's unavailable on weekends.

6. You don't know exactly where he lives.

7. He has a tan line or impression on his ring finger.

8. He has no social media presence.

9. He doesn't talk about his past relationships.

10. He pays for dates with cash. (Moore, 2016)

Surviving Working In A Hostile Work Environment

1. **Find an Escape** – Take a break away from the office. Go for a walk. Take a short vacation. Put up family pictures so that you have positivity in what you can control. If you can put on headphones, listen to relaxing music while you work. Avoid the abuser or the confrontations, when possible.

2. **Find Allies** – Involve like-minded coworkers in any or all of these three steps to share the burden: talk about it, discuss possible solutions and act as a group. If you can, as a group, draft a letter with action items to create a more positive atmosphere. (Thompson, 2016)

3. **Protect Yourself** – Become familiar with the company's policy related to the appropriate behaviors in the workplace and interactions. Keep records of all actions from the person causing the hostile work environment.

4. **Seek Help** – Talk to your manager about the situation. Be prepared to discuss what you have experienced. Provide incidents that have taken place. And, when letting them know, try to take the emotion out so that you don't sound petty. That what you are experiencing is serious and you need their help. If it is your manager that is causing the hostility, get human resources involved. Keep going up the chain until there is a resolution.

Bibliography

Coping With Grief. (2005). Retrieved from WebMd: http://www.webmd.com/ mental-health/mental-health-coping-with-grief

Davis, J. L. (2005). *Women Over 50: Your Personal Checklist.* Retrieved from WebMD: http://www.webmd.com/women/features/ women-over-50-your-personal-checklist#1

Dementia - Symptoms. (1995). Retrieved from WebMD: http://www.webmd.com/ alzheimers/tc/dementia-symptoms

Eye CandyCreations. (2017, August 8). Retrieved from Cynthia Bailey Eyewear: https://cynthiabaileyeyewear.com/sunwear/

Graham, J. (2013, March 07). *After the Caregiving Ends.* Retrieved from New York Times : http://newoldage.blogs.nytimes.com/2013/03/07/ after-the-caregiving-ends/

Martin, G. (1996). *O Romeo Romeo! Wherefore art thou Romeo ?* Retrieved from The Phrase Finder: http://www.phrases.org.uk/meanings/262200.html

Moore, J. D. (2016, August 8). *10 Warning Signs You May Be Dating A Married Man!* Retrieved from Couples Counseling Center: http://www. couplescounselingchicago.net/10-warning-signs-may-dating-married-man/

Phd, K. C. (2011, March). *Grief: Coping with the loss of your loved one.* Retrieved from American Psychological Association: http://www.apa.org/helpcenter/ grief.aspx

The Bible Study Site. (n.d.). Retrieved from http://www.biblestudy.org/bibleref/ meaning-of-numbers-in-bible/8.html

Thompson, M. (2016). *Ten Ways to Survive a Hostile Working Environment.* Retrieved from Hearst Newspaper Group: http://work.chron.com/ten-ways- survive-hostile-working-environment-1517.html

About the Author

Biography of Patricia A. Saunders

Self Published Author Patricia A. Saunders was born and raised in Connecticut before relocating to the San Francisco Bay Area nearly twenty-three years ago. She received her Master's in Management from the University of Phoenix in 2011. After the passing of her mother who had Alzheimer's, Patricia decided that all the words that she'd kept to herself were to be released.

Her work has been featured on a Coast to Coast Book Tour at the Los Angeles Times Festival of Books, Tucson Book Festival, Miami International Festival of Books and AARP Life@50+ Spring Convention. Also on In the Company of Poets, Women Owned Business Club Magazine, and Alysha Live! Radio Show and Coach Deb Bailey Secret of Success Talk Radio. She performs locally at spoken word events and Capital Jazz SuperCruise Open Mic with Grammy Award Winner Eric Roberson.

She is a monthly blogger of her own blog, Blessed & Curvy, who covers today's hot topics.

She released her first self-published book *Through the Fire* (March 2012) which covered situations, circumstances, and life lessons that have influenced her over her lifetime. On a mission to complete a book a year, she released her second book *Loving Me* (2013) and third *Let It Rain* (2014) which is also self-published and covers various topics from love, grief, self-image, self-esteem, bullying, and discovery of self-love. Her fourth book (2016) *This Too Shall Pass* was released by AuthorHouse Publishing and readers have given it a five-star rating.

In her spare time, Patricia enjoys writing poetry, traveling, spending time with family and wine tasting.

Her books are available at your local book retailers, at www.patriciaasaunders. com, www.amazon.com and www.barnesandnoble.com

You can follow her on social media:

Facebook: @blessedpoetpat

Twitter: @blessedpoetpat

Instagram: @blessedpoetpat

Pinterest: @blessedpoetpat
